21st Century Foundation and Principles

for

Socioeconomic Development and

Social Entrepreneurship

21st Century Foundation and Principles

for

Socioeconomic Development and

Social Entrepreneurship

Dr. Richard Corker-Caulker, ACSW, FACM

Order this book online at www.trafford.com
or email orders@trafford.com

Most Trafford titles are also available at major online book retailers.

To all social workers, churches and goverment workers

Printed in the United States of America.

ISBN: 978-1-4669-0119-3 (sc)
ISBN: 978-1-4669-0120-9 (hc)
ISBN: 978-1-4669-0121-6 (e)

Library of Congress Control Number: 2011918503

Trafford rev. 11/19/2012

 www.trafford.com

North America & international
toll-free: 1 888 232 4444 (USA & Canada)
phone: 250 383 6864 ♦ fax: 812 355 4082

Contents

The researcher hopes the information contained in this book will inspire many to rise and start living the life of dominion that God gave to all human kind for prosperity and peace.

Bible opens with a declaration, in Genesis1:1, that in the beginning God created the heavens and the earth. This spells out the relationship between God and the material world, including living and non living things. There seems to be a misunderstanding over the role of God in creating the material world and the identity of man as the image and likeness of God created to subdue the earth and it resources and have dominion. This misunderstanding has contributed to self-inflicted poverty, poor governance and limited role of institutions that put themselves out to represent God avoiding material development of the earth and it resources and good governance or dominion.

How long this misunderstanding is left to go on without correction will depend on the willingness to research this topic, the role of institutions on earth, and offer a new direction and responsibility in the role of religion in helping human beings subdue the earth and it resources and achieve dominion for all. Re-directing the role of religion is going to be critical as we see the collapse of political and socioeconomic institutions and structures around us and cuts in education, programs and services for helping children and family experience dominion and full identity development. Socioeconomic development will continue to dominate the world stage and affect youths until correct understanding of the human identity, ability and responsibility to subdue the earth and it resources and have dominion is built into religious or salvation, political, business thinking and practice.

The study you are going to read about was designed to investigate the facts about a generalization made by two church leaders about cuts made in church program and services for the poor in cities across United States of America. The researcher investigated and tested the claims made by the church leaders to determine whether the claims apply in the church field in Detroit, Michigan. Detroit was chosen because the university that the study proposed was closed and the researcher was familiar with the area because he worked in the city as a Field intern. Also, Detroit is a typical bustling economic center that was once a thriving city with thousands of people employed in America car industries. Detroit declined and many left the city and unemployment and poverty increased. Detroit experienced what many cities across America are experiencing in terms of unemployment and poverty and challenge for civic and church leaders. Learning how Detroit church leaders and civic leaders cope with a run-down city will generate the insight applicable in the Twenty-First century in cities across America and the world. While we may develop insight about how civic and church leaders respond to socioeconomic challenges in the 80's-90's we will understand that responding to individuals and families in economic depressed areas and cities is not about business, political and religious experience or creating jobs but is about developing the right theoretical insight about true human identity, abilities and equal dominion for all rooted in human communal quest for equal communal living. This is why learning from Detroit is important as well as developing the correct and appropriate theoretical foundation for socioeconomic development and social entrepreneurship for the Twenty-First century. Also, is about learning from a city, it population and leadership with incarnated experience.

The reason for researching the topic was fourfold. First, to find out whether not the church that participated in the study referred to here as the church provided programs, services and staff to meet the need of people in Detroit and how. Second, I was exposed to human spiritual and socioeconomic problems earlier in his ministry and studies in Africa, the Far East, Europe, and America, and wanted to research a topic that would give help explain the church response to socioeconomic problems and become the foundation of faith-based socioeconomic policies and social entrepreneurship in the 21st century. Third, as a researcher I want to contribute to the fundamental knowledge and theory of 21st century faith-based socioeconomic development and social entrepreneurship using biblical principles. Fourth, the researcher wants to improve the church's understanding of created resources and the problem of the fall of Adam and Eve as the foundation for faith-based socioeconomic development and social entrepreneurship for the 21st century.

The study was developed during the time the researcher was a seminary doctoral student in Michigan. The study was proposed in1997 and completed in 2000. The researcher proposed the study for his doctoral research for understanding the church response to socioeconomic challenges in city like Detroit, Michigan had hit by decline in the car industry and unemployment. Also, the researcher wanted to find out if the church had buildings, offices, staff, training and resources to respond to socioeconomic problems and poverty in the Detroit area and what sought of programs and services the church in the study was providing or not providing.

This question is still valid today in an economy hit by recession across the United States, Europe and in North America. It seems that individuals are looking to religious leaders as well as political leaders for leadership in socioeconomic issues and challenges including policy decision, programs and services that will affect changes and improve their life. This means that the role of religion can no longer be limited to spiritual development but should be comprehensive to touch all aspect of the human dimension including spiritual, mental, social and physical. Therefore, finding out how what the church in the study is doing and also developing a theoretical foundation for socioeconomic development and social entrepreneurship was the main focus of the study. But how consistent is the church response and the theoretical foundation with past attitude that church or religion should focus only on spiritual development and life after death concerns?

The researcher acknowledged past attempts by church leaders who wanted to find a possible solution to the long-held unresolved issues that have plagued the church over the use of church resources to support socioeconomic development and social entrepreneurship met resistance and sometime their studies and contribution to the age old problem of church and spirituality only was resisted. Because, the old school of theological interpretation of the condition of man in Genesis 1-3 was not comprehensive enough to take into account the whole person and systemic problems of Adam and Eve. Church leaders and theologians alike focus on the behavior, metaphysical and salvation concerns of the fall. But assessment of the Fall should be comprehensive to account for human identity as the image and likeness of God with responsibility to subdue the earth and it resources and the impact of sin on human identity, ability to subdue and have dominion and what can de done about it. This aspect is not generally a constituent part of theology and ministry.

Because, some religious leaders do not see the relationship between the fall of Adam and Eve giving rise to rehabilitation of the true identity of man as the image and likeness of God with on going responsibilities to subdue the earth and it resources and the exercise of dominion lacking among the poor as valid divine initiative resonating within the of Christian social involvement. Therefore, much earlier attempts to develop a theology like the social gospel and liberation theology developed to provide the theoretical foundation for social intervention was not received with open arms. The social gospel and liberation theology met strong opposition within the church. Some felt the social gospel and liberation theology were very liberal and extreme for conservative comforts. The Social Gospel movement emphasizes action on heaven on earth, while liberation theology supports Christian actions against oppressive governments and freedom. Liberation theology developed its foundation from the biblical story of the Exodus from Egypt. The social gospel called individuals to look for their heaven on the earth while at the same time waiting for millennial promises of the new earth and new heaven in the future. This meant the church not only playing spiritual role but will support and provide assistance to individuals necessary for better living.

The researcher is proposing a new approach from the book of Genesis, chapters 1 through 3, as the foundation for socioeconomic development and social entrepreneurship for the 21st century emphasizing socioeconomic development as a relationship than an economic activity and should include the development of human identity and recognizing the role of the human agent as the image and likeness of God with divine mission to continue subdue the earth and it resources for socioeconomic development, education, career choice, research, commerce, investment, economic recovery, job creation, innovation and technological advance and harm with training, knowledge and skills to respond not only to the spiritual and moral consequences of sin but the crisis index of problems associated with sin and it consequences for succeeding generation will have to face and cope with. Therefore, under this set of assessment of the true identity of fallen man, his duty to subdue the earth and it resources and claim dominion and at the same time face the consequences of sin the scope of religion needs to be broaden to resonate with the demand of human reality. This may not be an easy view to adopt but it worth the try than never if religion is to make sense to modern man.

Dedication

I would like to dedicate this book to my wife, Grace, and my daughters, Charis, Rachael, and Honoria. Also, I would like thank the Corker-Caulker descendants for their commitment and inspiration to improving the life of individuals. I must also not forget the men and women in the frontline of government, private, and business services who work to make policies and programs to create jobs, educate, protect, and care for others making sure every individual and family are learning about great opportunities in natural resources development and education and in developing the programs and services to respond to human crisis and challenges working for the benefit, peace and prosperity for all and those that will read and respond to the principles set forth in this book in their villages, towns and cities.

Foreword

This study was proposed during my seminary doctoral research in 1997 and completed in 2000. I wanted to be practical and to improve lives. I had already been exposed to human spiritual and socioeconomic problems in Africa, the Far East, Europe, and America. I believe people can be helped to become socioeconomically independent in a manner consistent with biblical and spiritual principles. I am glad the results of the study are now ready to be put in the hands of individuals, families, church leaders, business leaders, business students, theology students, political leaders, and socioeconomic developers.

At the time the study was proposed, it was viewed by some as being contrary to the theology, mission, and ministry of the church to be involved in socioeconomic development and entrepreneurship because some believe according to the popular belief that it is the responsibility of the state to educate individuals about human identity and dominion. Also, no one expect the researcher will be able to develop a Biblical theoretical foundation neutral from what has been done in the social gospel and liberation theology. Apparently, some Christians believe that God is only interested in spiritual matters and pays no attention to human material needs. This belief has created an attitude within the history of the church such that theology, mission, and ministry have been understood only within the context of spiritual matters. This belief and attitude has, in away, undermined any effort to reach people holistically.

We see this attitude not only in religion and theology but among business leaders and other professionals, who view the use of natural resources for the production of goods and services and use of human resources for hiring and labor outside the scope of spirituality. The same attitude also holds true for social workers and other program or service providers who view social work, human programs, and related services to be outside the scope of spirituality.

Someone has to take up the challenge to research these claims and to articulate a foundation for faith-based socioeconomic development and social entrepreneurship for the 21st century and then convince the church, business leaders, social workers, and government leaders to reconsider socioeconomic development as a holistic demand consistent with biblical principles for the 21st century.

Although this research is academic in the sense that is an attempt to rule out whether there is a decline in church programs and services for helping the poor, the topic is of such huge interest because socioeconomic realities affect every individual and family. If left unresolved, the present socioeconomic condition will continue to have the same impact it has always had on individuals and families. It will also continue to influence the attitude that poverty is due to poor judgment and to human laziness.

From this research, you willl earn that though poverty is relative, it can have many explanations, including, but not limited to, a lack of understanding of one true identity, divine dominion status, distance from natural resources, failure to invest in human resources, and failure to locate and stock pile adequate resources for crisis situations. Furthermore, from this study, you will see that poverty could be explained as a relationship problem in the three spheres of relationship: God------Man-------Material.

The core foundation for 21st century faith-based socioeconomic development is the awareness of one self as the image and likeness of God, given authorized divine responsibility to exercise dominion over the earth and its natural resources. Therefore, in order to reverse the trend of poverty and improve socioeconomic development in the 21st century, all children should be taught and exposed to this concept, including adults or families that have lost a sense of their identity and thus failed to hold dominion.

Until all socioeconomic development programs and services are stirred toward the direction of reviving the self-image of man and the restoration of dominion, the false beliefs that have undermined human identity, and left many without their dominion, will continue to rob succeeding generations of their identity and the link between their self-worth and their dominion.

The author looks at the human crisis, from the context of Adam and Eve, as a transgenerational problem that requires more complex responses than the church has ever acknowledged.

The call is grounded in the spiritual understanding of human kind's problem that began with humanity's first family. The call is to engage human problems that did not start with you and will not end with you.

The solution to human problems lies in cooperation with a higher power and the willingness to use biblical principles along side new ideas and theories of practice to become agents of change, restoring fallen humanity to its holistic image, fruitfulness, and dominion.

Therefore, solution to on going human needs and socioeconomic problems is not limited to a specific area of knowledge, profession, or trade, but is a responsibility of bringing about change in individuals not only by medical doctors, pastors, politicians, and social workers but by those who work in every profession. The church's part is not only to lead people to the Creator but also to teach individuals to love God and be responsible for there sources created by God, making sure that all have access and benefit from the natural resources created by Him.

The foundation of faith-based socioeconomic development lies in the recognition that God created the earth. In simple terms, God created mass. Mass is anything that has weight and occupies space and is made of matter. Matter exists in the form of liquids, solids, and gases.

God also created human being sin His image and likeness and gave human kind dominion over the things He created, both living and nonliving, including the human psychosocial environment.

The Bible states that in the beginning, God (spiritual being) created (an act) the heaven sand the earth. God created real places: heaven (study of astronomy) and the planet Earth with all component their parts, including life (the study of biology), chemistry, physics, earth sciences, materials, and human resources.

Therefore, Faith-based social services should seek to integrate spirituality, human resources, and material resources into socioeconomic development for solving human problems. Human beings should unite with God in His environment to utilize God's blessings.

A good response to human issues and problems requires two basic steps: The first step is trying to understand the problem from the individual's perspective. The second step is intervention. This is where you match the problem with material intervention. The solution or intervention to human problem is spiritual and material. To do one and exclude the other is a poor approach to human development. This study underscores a fundamental principle that religious, political, business, educational, families and individuals can no longer continue to isolate or fail to teach and preach about human identity and it link to socioeconomic development and entrepreneurship.

Because, true religion, government, education, socioeconomic, entrepreneurship and the helping professions can only occurred in the context and environment of full awareness of true human identity and the divine and natural responsibilities associated with that identity to subdue the earth and it resources and to have dominion or govern and rule the earth.

The issue is how important and relevant is the identity of man and the responsibilities that resonate with that identity in to days religious, political, educational and socioeconomic leadership and development? Well, if you have been watching news headlines and not just football or paying no attention you will see around the globe and in your own backyard news media and people old and young calling attention to this very issues in cities, towns, countries and nations were neglect of individuals and families have continue for decades and majority of citizens have to take to the street demanding access to land, food, jobs, education, health services, clean environment, water, energy and new laws that will enforced how we treat human beings and create opportunities for individuals and families to have shared access to opportunities and affordable goods and services. It comes as no surprise God at creation created an environment in space with all the natural resources man will need to survive. Why should that not be part of religious, political, family round table and educational concern and discussion? In the next chapter, we will limit our discussion to the specific problem this study was designed to explore.

Chapter One

The Problem

The name of the denomination or church the research was completed has been deleted for confidential reasons. Therefore, the word church, members, leaders, former president, Gavin and Sahlin will be used to represent the denomination. The problem we are trying to address is, Gavin former assistant director of the church development agency, traced the historical church's commitment to the poor back to World War I. The church provided food, clothing, and work opportunities to needy families; however, Gavin discovered that the church that was active in her commitment to the poor during World War 1 has declined in her commitment to the welfare ministry of the Church.[1]

Sahlin, former director of the church development and relief services, described major cuts in workforce and programs in many North American community service centers 1988, with few leaders or directors for community services on a half-time basis.[2]

Community ministry served as an umbrella for the organization and was always under the umbrella of the local churches and conferences in the United States, Canada, and Bermuda operating a wide variety of social services, including health screening and education, family life workshops, meals and shelters for the homeless, assistance with immigration issues, disaster relief, and other activities.[3]

Is the observation and report by Gavin and Sahlin applicable in the Michigan church Conference?

The Problem

Hypothesis 1

Theological dualism is a contributing factor to decline in faith-based program evident by cut in staff, community services and programs for the poor.

Is theological dualism responsible for the decline in programs and services in the church?

Hypothesis 2

Narrow theological assessment and understanding of Adam and Eve identity and dominion is the cause for limiting the scope of the theology, mission and ministry of the church.

The question is, is the lack of understanding of Adam Eve identity and dominion responsible for limiting the theology, teaching, preaching, mission and ministry only to spiritual problem?

Hypothesis 3

A holistic, comprehensive assessment and understanding of the Genesis human identity, dominion, problems and challenges increase level of motivation, commitment and training in socioeconomic development and entrepreneurship.

The question is will the increase understand of integration of Genesis chapter 1-3 increase commitment to faith-based social services training, program and services?

Justification for the study

In the wake of cuts in community social services observed by Sahlin and Gavin completing a field study of the problem for understanding the situation is a positive sign. The result of the study will also rule out whether the generalization applies or not.

Social problems may create challenges and opportunities for religious organizations to impact their communities.[4]

In 1997, the church General Conference sensed the need for dialogue in the areas of missions and social action. High-ranking officials in the Church, representatives from the church Development and Relief Agency, and professors from the church university in Michigan met to discuss the church and it response to social problems[5]

The need to develop a socioeconomic principle based on biblical foundation for entrepreneurship and faith-based community programs and social services for church is urgently needed because of the socioeconomic challenges confronting mankind and the harsh realities of business practices and social programs and services that misuse vital resources for purpose unintended.

The study will bring together information for and against faith-based socioeconomic development and social entrepreneurship and the foundation and principle for faith-based socioeconomic practice all in one research. This will contribute knowledge to the field.

Limitations of the Research

The report only represents the responses of thirty church leaders that participated in the study. The data do not include all the churches in the conference but a reasonable number necessary for analysis.

Research Methodology

The field study was designed to find out if the decline mentioned by Sahlin and Gavin applies to churches in the Michigan Conference.

A questionnaire was developed and mailed out to church conference secretary in Michigan for distribution. Several variables were included.

A qualitative designed was used in the study. Qualitative methods have different meanings for different people, depending on a person's intellectual background. A qualitative approach is largely an inductive process used by a scientist or researcher to attempt to gain an understanding of the patterned meanings, perceptions, beliefs, values, and behaviors of a particular group of people in relationship to a research problem (Carlson, Robert., Siegal, H., and Falck, R. 1995)[6]. Qualitative research studies things, situations, problems or phenomena. It is also used to find out what people do, know, think, and feel about their condition, problem, or issue in a thematic descriptive way, differing from existing information, theory, explanation, or generalization.

The data was collected and analyzed. Then, a coordinated effort was used to support the response. Qualitative steps include the following: find out what you want to learn about, ask questions, decide who you are going to ask and how, gather the data, analyze the data using word processor and write what you have found out about the question.[7]

Chapter Two

Political Theories for Government-run Social Programs

The issue all ways surface are again and again whose responsibility is it to lead socioeconomic development and social entrepreneurship and who will be good at it? Arguably, some will hint the state is responsible and will be good at taking the lead to invest in human and natural resources for socioeconomic development, education, research and entrepreneurship developing policies, programs and services that will respond to human problems like health and medical issues etc. This response may not hold true for religious followers with conviction that the world was created by God including humans and humans were handed a responsibility to subdue the earth and it resources for meaningful use, education, and research and job creation consistent with human dominion on the earth. As long as this debate continues people will continue to see need for religious leaders and political leaders responsible for socioeconomic development even though leaders of this two great institution may not see a need or any relevance of their responsibility to lead and teach socioeconomic development and social entrepreneurship, dominion or governance or rule for benefit of all. Therefore, what do we know about the involvement of church and state in providing socioeconomic development and social entrepreneurship?

What are the spiritual and political responsibilities of society towards the poor? In this study, the researcher reviewed two current worldviews as a starting point for understanding dichotomy, Some church leaders believed the church is responsible only for spiritual problems and the political leadership for physical and social needs and development. In this chapter, the researcher will discuss the political worldview or theories of the Republican, Democratic and Liberal political groups in the United States.Second, the researcher will describe the Michigan State-owned socioeconomic programs and services for the poor and those in need. The reason for discussing Michigan's response to the poor in need is that the church that is the focus of the study resides in Michigan. Therefore, understanding the state's response will give us an idea to evaluate, on one hand, how the state is responding, and on the other hand, how the church in the study is responding.

We all live in an economy that has been constructed by the powerful and wealthy. The economy we have created from Adam and Eve is built on a particular political and socioeconomic philosophy.

Social Democrats

Social Democrats believe that poverty and social problems are caused by a conflict in social values. Conflict means a contested struggle among groups or institutions with opposite aims and perspectives.

Therefore, restoring order will bring about equilibrium, stability, continuity, consensus, integration, and social control. Government intervention is always inevitable to create access for all, because Social Democrats believe that competing powers and different aims will create a disequilibrium in society and the day-to-day lives of people.

Because of this disequilibrium, the government needs to intervene on behalf of the oppressed, the poor, the working class, and the middle class that cannot compete for goods or services, as well as those who have been bypassed, excluded, or prevented from achieving successful human development.

This belief is clearly articulated in programs and services aimed at the poor, the needy, and the deprived. Social Democrats do not argue against the control and accumulation of resources or against capitalism.

Neoconservative

The neoconservative believes that a welfare state and welfare programs will eventually fracture traditional family life, erode the work ethic, and legitimize unearned leisure time without shame or penalty. Therefore, government should cut down on social programs and services that do not encourage economic independence.

The logic is that people who receive state benefits and free programs will do nothing about ending their dependence. The neoconservative view states that individuals are responsible for their own poverty. Therefore, investing in programs that encourage the individual to be independent could result in eradicating poverty and dependence.

Neoconservatives are mainly responsible for advocating that government should stay out of people's lives and pockets, while at the same time advocating the control of resources and services by the wealthy rather than by the masses. They are prepared to fight any legislation that will empower the masses or restore the masses to a position of dominion over the few.

They believe the few should continue to be incharge of controlling all resources and services through democratic capitalism. They reject the idea that material resources are existential resources never created for democratic capitalism, a capitalism that says getting a hed of everyone else or becoming rich at the expense of others is just fine so long as there are no laws against it.Democratic capitalism, however effective it may appear, has its merits and demerits and has been one of the leading causes of the modern economic collapse, greed, stagnation, and poor development, as well as the creation of a few people in the wealthy class at the same time that masses are living in poverty.

Liberals

Liberals, on the other hand, believe society needs reform in order to enable those who are less privileged to climb up. Liberals also share the opinion that if the government doesn't intervene, the result will be disorganization and social stress. If poverty is allowed to go unchecked, it will trigger all sorts of vices, as well as disease, mental unrest, family breakdown, crime, and social problems. In the liberal view, the function of the state is to modify the negative aspects of capitalism. Capitalism, however effective, has a down side, and it is the duty of government to minimize the problems of capitalism.

One of the great argument levied against political parties and leadership in leading out socioeconomic development and social entrepreneurship stems from the observation that some times political leadership may not see a need to be involve in the market because of the attitude the market can operate better when it is free from speculated legislation that may limit business ventures or drive business to places of the world were there are less and less rule or government leadership is free to involve in business or use national resources human or natural to make money for themselves that leading. This attitude may guarantee freedom to business leaders but evidence in the twenty-first century shows nations have been left abandoned to fend for themselves while the political elites are making use of human and natural resources to create family and personal wealth than wealth for all and for the nation. Others have exploited the free-for-all to exploit and profiteer at the expense of the wider population or paying themselves or share holders more money for lavish life style than rewarding those who contributed to bring the income and making the business successful. This is why in an attempt to stamp out the worst of human nature individuals are calling for a fair playing field and reward for all because, too many are not getting equal pay or less for equal labor and sharing of profit. Also, many have been left behind or have not seen their pay rise or fired form their job or laid-off because it is better to cut work force and spend lees make a lot of profit while few take on all the work for many. Also, the world has come to realize the economy of the 19-20th centuries benefited few families that have control of human resources and natural resources and use it well to stack-up wealth for themselves at the expense of the wealth for all. Great majority of people did not thrived and many lost jobs, due to lack of investment in human resources development and natural resources to create jobs and fair share of earned business profit made through combination of human and natural resources. Some convert their economy from manufacturing and production to market economy selling what others have made from subduing natural resources. The trend of relying on few to produce for many will continue until leaders discover a relationship between human identity, spiritual responsibilities, economic activities, entrepreneurship and dominion or governance as part of a whole.

As a result cities ran down, unemployment kicked in emotional issues like disappointment, frustration and depression crept in on many unexpectedly around the world and medical conditions worsen as many can not afford daily living let alone medical expenses many live for months and decades without their medical needs address and moral integrity slips and the concept of we are brothers, the image likeness of God with shared dominion eluded many because it was never incorporated and translated in the teachings of society because some states and religious leadership did not create a society knowingly and unknowingly a society of equal dignity of every child with dominion instead created class of upper and lower individuals and families for decades with less and less laws, programs and services to equalize communities. How did political leadership respond to socioeconomic challenges in Detroit, Michigan, the city or field of this study? Let us take a look at this first and then move to the church in Michigan this study was designed to study.

Chapter Three

Michigan State Social Programs and Services

Until the 1900s, community social service programs were the exclusive concern of private organizations, particularly churches. The Protestant churches took the lead in providing faith-based community social services. Protestant churches later cut back on social service efforts when Franklin D. Roosevelt became president of the United States.

Roosevelt's dream was that even though the federal government could not ensure 100 percent of the population against 100 percent of the risks and vicissitudes of life, the Social Security policy would give some measure of protection to the average citizen and his or her family against the loss of a job, health problems, and poverty in old age.[8]

The Social Security program was introduced by the federal government. The program cost citizens' work-time savings that involves paying certain percentage of income earned back by contribution from your employer. The policy requires universal coverage and compulsory deductions must be made directly from each worker's salary.[9]

In exchange for each worker's monthly contribution, the government promises to provide retirement, survivor benefits, unemployment benefits, disability benefits, and Medicare health insurance. Social Security programs and services provide some assistance to help individuals during periods of heat or other adverse weather conditions, as well as providing family planning, antipoverty programs, neighborhood health centers, and mental health services.[10]

Medical and public health programs provide treatment for and prevention of diseases and injuries, as well as substance abuse treatment necessary to protect life or private safety.[11]

This is one way to fight back against poverty in old age, which is a fact of life no matter your past work contribution or savings. We have to remember that in states with a higher population of mothers, children, students, and the elderly, those who are unemployed are at higher risk of poverty.Today, even the safety net of Social Security funds will not be enough to pay for all services. Therefore, individuals are advised to invest in private retirement funds. However, due to recent negative experiences and the Wall Street collapse in 1999, many investors and potential investors are left wondering about relying on these investment funds for future economic security.

The researcher has included in this chapter a description of the social problems of Detroit, Michigan, as a background to the problems confronting many poor in cities around the world. Furthermore, the problem provides an example of the social problems confronting all urban churches. This example will provide a tool for evaluating the response of the church in this study. The following data reflect information available from 1980 to 1990. Detroit, a major city in Michigan's industrial development, was ruined, abandoned, decayed, or destroyed in that decade.

The annual population in Detroit declined 14.6 percent between 1980 and 1990 and again by 3.5 percent between 1990 and 1994. The population was 1,027,974, according to the 1990 census. By 2000, the census put the population at 951,270, a 7.5 percent drop, although the city disagreed with the report (Mayor's Press Release by US Census Bureau, 2000). At the same time, median household income was $18,742 in 1990. The cost of health care per month per family was $567 inthecity.

The census also reported that 59 percent of mothers with children six years old or younger were in the labor force. There were 71,876 children living with a mother as the only parent, while 9,343 children were being parented only by a father. It is no surprise that with the decline in jobs, falling income, an increase in parenting problems, and less supervised care, social problems and poverty multiply. Other social problems that also emerged were homelessness and poverty. The poverty and unemployment in Detroit has been in the making for decades as society misunderstood the true human identity, abilities to subdue the earth and it resources and maintain dominion as vital part of natural human development.

Therefore, The situation in 2010 may not be any better for the poor in the city all of a sudden or twinkle of an eye let alone in the world, as man continues to face challenging environmental and economic problems and issues. Michigan State has been responding to social problems and socioeconomic challenges in Detroit by programs and social service. Are the Michigan State social programs and services similar or deferent from the church in the field study? We will not know the answer to the question just yet until we go over chapter seven and start discussing the data from the field study.

Michigan Child Program

The Michigan Child program gets its name from Michigan Children's Health Programs. (MI Child is pronounced "mychild.") This program provides services and medical coverage for all children of working people for only $5 per month, regardless of family size.[12]

This program targets families with no health insurance and a monthly income of less than $1,800 for a family of two, $2,300 for a family of three, $2,800 for a family of four, or $3,200 for a family of five.[5] Michigan Child focuses on prevention better than on traditional corrective services.[13]

Aid to Families with Dependent Children (AFDC)

State and local authorities provide health, education, food stamps, Medicaid or Medicare, and disability and unemployment benefits. In 1993, Wayne County (the Detroit area) provided benefits to 288,924 people or families who needed them.[14] The County also provided medical check-ups, shots, emergency dental care, prescription pharmaceuticals, hospital care, prenatal care and delivery, and vision and hearing benefits.[15] Services are also available that provided checkups, shots, emergency dental care, pharmaceuticals, hospital care, prenatal care and delivery, and vision and hearing benefits.[16]

Chapter Four

Legacy of Dualism

Should we expect the Christian church to develop practices of theology, teaching, mission, and ministry that will provide similar services to individuals and families? The church in North America attempted in the past to provide a theological foundation for social entrepreneurship that was called the social gospel. The social gospel was an attempt to make Christianity more relevant to individual social and economic concerns by addressing human needs in the contemporary world. The view was that while looking for a heaven in which the soul returns to unite with God, the earth can be a place also to live like in heaven while awaiting the arrival of the return of Christ.

For very long church leaders have seen the danger and risk of making religion only about spiritual matter while excluding all other dimension of God as the creator that created human being not only to obey, worship him and serve God but also created to be responsible for the things God created to subdue the earth and it resources and to have dominion. Any extreme move to view the role of religion only as spiritual matter to the exclusion of the other dimension of man will undermine meaningful responsibility to obey, worship and serve God and also to develop the earth and the resources God has entrusted to man as part of his dominion. Those who have been tempted to limit the role of man to spiritual matter have done so at the expense of socioeconomic development and entrepreneurship. Religion has become an instrument of debate, ideological conflict between those perceiving they represent God and those who do not. Also, religion has been use to fuel conflict between religion living socioeconomic concerns aside. Some believe God will come and work on the earth and resources for them while there duty is complete silence over human identity and dominion.

The theology of the social gospel by Niebuhr[17] and Rauschenbusch[18] was criticized by many who viewed their theological emphasis as undermining the main thrust of the gospel, which is to save soul. Does the Bible promote a hierarchy of salvation? To help answer the question and determine the

11

origin of the hierarchy of salvation, the following literature was reviewed to give an idea about what is already known.

According to the literature, the origin of Western dualism can be traced to a philosophical system developed at Alexandria, Egypt, in the third century by Plotinus (205-270 CE) and his successors.[19] Plotinus constructed an elaborate hierarchy of spiritual levels through which the soul can ascend from physical existence to an eventual merging with the Divine. This represents traditional Greek rationalism of a scheme of salvation: the merging of self or soul into a higher life. The order includes the one, divine, physical world and the soul that supports this finite and visible world, which includes the individual and all matter. Although the school was closed by Justin the Christian in AD 529, Platonism has grown. Platonism lived on and exhibited. Platonism has grown. Platonism lived on and exhibited its influence in the views of Christian leaders who tended to prioritize Christian theology, belief, teaching, training, mission, and ministry to exclude anything that is matter or physical from Christian teaching, mission, and ministry. Furthermore, the world at large tends to separate. Platonism has grown. Platonism lived on and exhibited its influence in the views of Christian leaders who tended to prioritize Christian theology, belief, teaching, training, mission, and ministry to exclude anything that is matter or physical from Christian teaching, mission, and ministry. Furthermore, the world at large tends to separate.

To conclude this chapter on dualism it is important to share that in the Egyptian priestly office priest were only limited to serve the God the represent and to offer sacrifice to the God so the God can be please to bring good things harvest, fortune and prevent farming and drought etc. But the Egyptian priestly office did seek material blessing for the people but through the Gods. The people and the priest expect material blessings comes form their Gods. But in the Hebrew culture priest were not only trained in sacred things but also learn different trade. Jesus is one example of a spiritual leader with knowledge and skills on how to access wood and make furniture. Jesus did not expect people to sit and wait for God to access natural resources for socioeconomic development and job creation. Jesus employed himself by accessing natural resources and human resources to produce goods and services consistent with the dominion of man. All dimension of man is equally important.

The importance of beliefs cannot be overemphasized, because beliefs have the power to either improve or limit your development and involvement with the world and what you may consider relevant or a priority. Beliefs may also influence your thoughts, attitudes, feelings, behavior, or involvement with the world, or they can separate you from the world and its resources.

The literature shows that the Western religious worldview has been influenced by the Greek worldview that separated the body and the sprit. Elmore, a Christian writer, described this separation as the distinction between one's body and one's soul.[20] Elmore traced the dichotomy of the Western worldview to Plato, who made a distinction between man's material and spiritual dimensions in Neoplatonism.

Neoplatonism is a philosophical and religious system that both rivaled and influenced Christianity from the 3rd to the 6th century, and was derived from the work of the Greek philosopher Plato (427-347 BCE) along with elements of oriental mysticism. The founder of Neoplatonism was Plotinus (205-270 CE), who constructed an elaborate hierarchy of spiritual levels through which the individual soul could ascend from physical existence to merge with the One. Interest in Neoplatonic philosophy, sometimes associated with magic and demonology, was revived in the period called the Renaissance.[21]

Neoplatonism dominated the Greek philosophical schools and remained powerfully influential until the teaching of philosophy by pagans ended in the late 6th century. Neoplatonism postulated an all-sufficient unity, the One, from which emanated the Divine Mind, or Logos, and below that, the World Soul. Those transcendent realities were thought to support the visible world. All thing semanated from the One, and individual souls could rise to mystical union with the One through contemplation.

The real world, in Plato's mind, is the invisible world. The visible world on Earth is simply an image of the real world, like a shadow world projected on the wall of a cave.[22]

Plato believed that the physical world with its property represents an imperfect reproduction of its counterpart in the spiritual world.[23] Humans have an immortal spirit. Therefore, the spiritual life is of greater importance than one's physical body or material needs.

Elmo reconcluded that Plato's dualism influenced the Christian church fathers and theologians and, inturn, influences the focus and scope of Christian ministry. It will also set the stage for all successive debates on what is relevant and not relevant for the church as it interacts with individuals and communities.[24]

Lee, a Christian writer, identified the Hellenistic philosophical influence on Greeks and Christian church leaders. First, Greek philosophers on the

Greek mainland emphasized the importance of the human spirit. Second, Ionian materialists, a group of philosophers, emphasized that matter is all there is and denied the existence of sprit and deity, regarded humans as exclusively corporeal, and denied the very existence of a soul or spiritual entity.[25]

Elmore identified particular Christian church leaders who may have been influenced by Greek philosophical world views. In the first group, he includes those who believe that a human being essentially consists of three dimensions: a body, a soul, and a inmaterial spirit (which is peculiarly human).[25] Clement of Alexandria, Origen, Gregory of Nyssa, Deliztsch, and Oehlerall belong to this group of thought. The second group divided the human into a material body and an indestructible soul.[26] In this group we have Athanasius, Augustine, and nearly all of the Reformers. Greek philosophy prioritized the person (orself) as an aspect of a human being, transcending and disparaging the body as a temporary shell that was not really part of the person.[27]

During the fourth century, Neoplatonism became the favored Western pagan creed that rivaled and influenced Christianity from the 3rd to the 6th century. It influenced Augustine and mediaeval Western theology.[28]

None of the references cited so far have shown how the Greek world view influenced Christian theology. However, Ferguson and Wright demonstrated how Christian church fathers were influenced. Greek Neoplatonism proved enormously attractive to Christian thinkers from Origin's succession onward.[29] The theologies of Ambrose, Victorianus, Austin, and Dionysius were also influenced by Neoplatonism, which became the most formative factor in Christian mystical theology in both the East and the West.

Neoplatonism influenced the theological writings of the Reformation period and Anglicanism, particularly from Hooker through the Cambridge Platonist, socialists to B.F. West Coot, John Bailey, Tillich, and the philosopher Iris Murdoch.[30]

John Sachs states that orientation that makes a distinction between the body and soul of a person inorder of importance dates back to ancient Greek philosophy (especially the various forms of Platonism and subsequent cultural and philosophical development in the West, particularly Descartes) rather than to a biblical understanding of the human person at creation.[31]

Chapter Five

Dualism and the Church

Has the church been prevented from doing a lot more for society because of dualism? Is your church practicing the prioritizing of salvation like pagan Greeks and how is your church doing that? Is your church teaching and preaching about the creator and created things?

Evangelical v Ecumenical Response

The Christian church in North America witnessed a decline in community social ministry after President Franklin D. Roosevelt initiated state-sponsored social services. Prior to these new programs, the church was active in providing social services until some leading churches prioritized the soul over the physical and social needs of Individuals.

Some felt it is the duty of the state to provide resources for physical and social needs. Also, the social gospel theology was seriously undermined by church leaders and theologians knowingly and unknowingly influenced by Greek world view and practice of prioritizing salvation contrary to the intent and act of God in creating the physical world, it resources and after man giving dominion over the physical world.

I was with a theologian who believed that after the fall man lost his dominion therefore should have no dominion over any created things. The role of the church now is to emphasize spirituality and nothing else because when Individuals accept Jesus Christ they will have everything even when they are not told about their dominion.

Since the U.S. government got involved in providing social services and programs the church has taking a leave and made spiritual problems and issues it major concern and goal. Some church leaders are comfortable with providing spiritual support and concluded the government, not the church, is responsible for meeting the material needs of individuals.

Where does the church stand in the debate? The literature search showed Evangelical and Eccumenical are divided on the issue. Where do you stand? It is possible when you are not a Christian leaders you are unconsciously following the Greek mindset of separating or creating a wall between your physical world and your spiritual world or perhaps thinking your professional belief, theories and practice must be kept separate from all other dimension of life. This false dichotomy still persists today.

Moberg, a Christian author, highlights the historical influence of dualism on present Christian mission by stating the fact that tension exists in the area of church and society. Some in the evangelical branch of Christianity in North America have built a stronger case for evangelism than direct social involvement[32] because Evangelicals tends to focus on the importance of the soul and the salvation of the soul over the physical body and needs. Other Evangelical visualizing the demerit of this orientation and practice has been taking parts in debate like abortion etc to show interest in human social and physical problems.

On the other hand, the so-called ecumenical wing of Protestant Christianity is the body of Christians who emphasizes social involvement, while evangelicals stress evangelism.[33] The current tension between evangelical and ecumenical is a continuation of a fundamentalist–modernist controversy.[34]

This controversy includes the church perspective on the world, human beings in their environment, and the role of the church in the community. It is important to understand that your future development and progress are linked to and will be shaped by your spiritual beliefs about what is relevant and important in your environment. Beliefs also affect your commitment and mission to serve.

Evangelical tends to favor converting individuals to the church, preparing them for life in the hereafter, and being rewarded salvation. Ecumenical, on the other hand, focuses on salvation, social services, and programs.

However, there seems to be a movement within evangelical circles that is attempting to integrate spirituality and social issues, such as faith and politics (for example, the question of abortion and when life starts).

Ronald J. Snider directs attention to a statement made by the Reverend Billy Graham, a leading evangelical, in 1966 at the World Congress on Evangelism. Graham said that this cause of evangelism (Gospel preaching) to which he (Graham) had dedicated his life was suffering from confusion.[35]

Snider throws some light on the perceived confusion. It occurred when biblical evangelism, which demands a personal confrontation with the claims of Jesus, retained the name *evangelism* but substituted another practice—the new evangelism—with an attempt to apply Christian principles to social order.[36]

This confusion was also mentioned in 1982 at the meeting of some fifty evangelical leaders from six continents who attended the Reformed Bible College consultation on the relationship between evangelism and social responsibility.

The meeting was cosponsored by the Louisiana Committee for World Evangelism and World Evangelical Fellowship. The members emphasized that the supreme and ultimate need of all mankind is the saving grace of Jesus Christ.

A person's eternal needs and salvation are of greater importance than his temporal, social, or material well being.[37] This statement sound theoretical; however, it has a practical implication for faith-based socioeconomic development and social entrepreneurship. To help us understand the practical issues, Bradshaw, a Christian mission author, cites one example of a Christian group that was arguing over relief work and gospel work. One group valued separation of Christian mission and ministry from social problems. Other members of the group valued a holistic approach to Christian mission and ministry and felt that gospel preaching and social problems must go hand-in-hand.[38] Bradshaw states that this present gap between man's physical and spiritual life is established by a false, theological dichotomy. The source of this dichotomy lies in the confrontation between the western world view and the biblical world view.

Bradshaw states that the biblical worldview is holistic, but western theological worldview is dualistic. This separation makes systematic theology and redemption a spiritual concern and leads one to assume that the non-spiritual needs of life belong to political leaders.[39]

It has not only affected the church but has affected every aspect of our life with false dichotomy. We struggle to maintain the dichotomy in our professional belief and practice and life style. We fail to see a connection between the natural world, it resources, the human being in his natural environment, human responsibility and dominion over the earth and it resources including responsible use of human resources.

Chapter Six

Specific Perspective

How has this controversy in dualism affected the church in the center of this study? Is the church involved in any dialogue to discuss man's dominion and the resources of nature in it theological training, mission and ministry. Also, what is the responsibility of the church leaders and members in investing and developing created things God created for human dominion?

Badillo, a church leader, described the ongoing influence of dualism in the church in America. He states some church leaders believe that neither Christ nor his disciples gave instruction regarding the church's responsibility toward social problems.[40]

L. A. Smith, writing in the Church magazine in 1905, said that Christians ought to rid their minds of the unrealistic idea that the principle of God's government would prevail in earthly government. He called on Christians not to devote time, energy, and resources to reform society or respond to social problems.[41]

Smith concluded that Christian mission was to preach and save souls. Therefore, any attempt on the part Church leaders to respond to social problems was considered a waste of means and resources needed in the cause of proclaiming Christ.[42]

Society and its problems, he thought, could be eliminated or reduced by preaching the gospel to every creature until the gospel message has been heard in all the world.[43] The prevalent belief was that it was the state's responsibility to respond to social problems and non-spiritual needs of individuals.

A key issue is whether the church has an obligation to or should provide faith-based social services to people with social problems and needs. There is no easy answer to this question taking into account present theological tension and division over the issue.

However, the literature reviewed showed several responses from churches in the past that will help us understand how church leaders responded to social problems in the late eighteen hundreds and early nineteen hundreds.

Butler, a church author contributing to the church magazine described the traditional church response. First, refers to members who may prefer to preach the gospel to a sinful world because nothing remedies human problems better than for people to hear the gospel and respond. Second, the church can help to eradicate poverty and save a community from its social evils.[44]

Tyner, another church leader, identified three other church responses. First, the Church may throw up its hands and turn its back on the world. Second, it may partially withdraw from the world, maintaining minimum contact with the larger society while awaiting the Second Advent. Third, it may accept the biblical mandate and respond by relating to the world in such a manner as to display the most attractive light.[45]

Linthicum, a church leader, described three different perspectives and responses. First, a church may think that because it is in a city and is a part of the community, it should not be involved with the community on solving social problems. It sees itself as "in" but not "of" the city.[46]

Second, a church may perceived itself as a church "to" the city and the community. This church realizes that if it does not interact with its geographical community in some way, it is going to die.[47] The temptation for this church is to decide what is best for the community without getting the community involved.

Third, the church may perceive itself as a church of the community, a church that is "with" the city or families. Therefore, the church then identifies and develops relationships with its community.[48]

Historically, the church had tended to shift its responses as it changes belief. However, some church leaders realized the importance of meeting man's holistic needs and developed a theology on welfare ministry in the eighteen hundreds.[49]

In the General Conference session of world leaders in 1888, the delegates heard the report of the church's pride in having twenty-two city ministries operating in response to social problems in American cities.[50]

Chicago became the laboratory for the church community-ministry programs. The goal of the program was to improve urban, slum-population problems and to provide lodging, penny lunches, nurse visits, Bible studies, and clothing distribution.[51]

Chilson and Preas, church instructors, concluded that social welfare ministries and services in the community are significantly influenced by the interest of the hierarchical system of the current religious body.[52]

Chilson and Preas help us understand how the interest of church leaders from time to time will affect whether a church gets involved in community action or just stay with spiritual programs.[53]

In 1998, an article in the church's Review cited a decline in the church support for community social ministries in centers in the North American Church Division. This decline was evident by cut in community social ministry workforce in many centers across North America. It is not clear whether this decline was due to a change in belief or a lack of interest in support of faith-based social services.

However, in 1988, a series of articles written by Church leaders appeared in the *church Review* in support of programs and services for the poor.

Drawing the attention of the church to the plight of the poor, a member wrote that every evening in North America thousands of men, women, and children do not go home but instead sleep on the streets or seek refuge in a shelter for the poor.[54]

The same member posed the questions: Should the church help? Isn't the mission of the church to preach the gospel? Does the Church have a worldwide task to fulfill? If we get involved with helping the needy, will the church be sidetracked from the Lord's commission? And, will the Church become merely a social organization that happens to keep the Sabbath? [55]

In response to these questions, the member took the position that God is the creator and sustainer of the universe and that healing and preaching were inseparable for Jesus.[56] The Old and New Testaments to support his position. He encouraged church members to continue showing social concern, spreading the gospel, developing medical and dental clinics, feeding the hungry, and clothing the naked[57]

A former president of the North American Division of the church asked if a caring church could do less than address the need in the face of world hunger. What is the caring church strategy all about if not the care of the people in need? [58]

The former president felt that when Jesus fed the five thousand, there were no doubt thousands, maybe millions, still hungry in the world. Caring is an attitude; Jesus' attitude was that the caring church must always turn the face of compassion to the needy.[59]

Another church member described how the Church helps millions of victims of poverty, victims of hunger, and victims of disaster every year, with specific countries benefiting from the church assistance. The activities of church Community Services of North America (ACS) involved six networks of 550 local centers staffed by volunteers who assisted nearly 3 million person annually.[60] Centers developed individualized assistance in response to local community needs.

Programs in the centers are focused on four types of services: clothing, food, disaster relief, and family services.[61] He concluded his article with a description of the church Development Relief Agency. He described the Relief Agency as a global agency that centered its assistance in seven distinct areas: human need; working with families, mothers, and children; improving community farming practices; developing better water resources; training for self-sufficiency; providing community-supported programs; and building and equipping communities and institutions.[62]

Another former president of the church General Conference explained the link between the church global strategy and the poor. He explained the fifty-eight chapters of Isaiah link the Sabbath directly to work on behalf of the less fortunate—to loose the bands of wickedness, to deal thy bread to the hungry, to bring the poor that are cast out to thy house, and to cover the naked. He concluded that in the history of the Church, medical missionary services have often been the "entering wedge" for church work in new places.[63]

In response to the biblical, theological, and historical confusion over the church's responsibility, a former General Conference vice president of the church stated that many have been confused by the warning against assisting the poor to the neglect of the "cause of God."[64]

He explained that some have concluded that the prophetess (referring to Ellen, a pioneer leader of the church in 1844) thought of work for the poor as something other than "the work of God,"—a responsibility subordinate to the main task of the church.[65]

A senior pastor of the Berean Church in Los Angeles, California, addressed another issue—the issue of commitment. He felt that the church has resources to effect change and cure but does not seem to have the commitment.[66] Failure to understand the holistic integration of Genesis chapter 1-3 may be responsible for the lack of commitment to faith-based social services may have been responsible for the decline in community social ministry.

But is this lack of commitment evident in the field study? Do we also have a decline in programs and services mentioned by Sahlin and Gavin? What do the result of the field investigation completed in 2000 show?

Chapter Seven

Field Study Report

A research matrix was utilized to analyze independent and dependent variables. Instead of a standardized test instrument, a research test instrument (or questionnaire) was adapted and used. The research question was designed to find out whether the generalization of Sahlin and Gavin apply in the Detroit churches of the church Conference. Also, the researcher wanted to find out if the churches are divided on support for and against faith-based services and whether the division is influenced by theological belief.

The sample size expected to participate in the study was sixty. The researcher wanted as many church leaders and providers of services to respond. Sixty questionnaires were mailed out. Sample size in qualitative research is generally about 5-25. The sample size depends on what the researcher wanted to know, pursue, or learn about.

The questionnaire was sent to the Michigan Conference secretary of the church for distribution to pastors and community ministry leaders. Other copies of the questionnaire were also sent to the director of the Van Ministry in Detroit, a ministry that provides health checks in the Detroit area. Return envelopes were provided.

The respondents in the study came from urban, suburban, and rural churches. Twenty-one were males, and nine were females; educational backgrounds ranged from high school to doctorate degrees.

Some had twenty years of employment in the church, while others had twenty-one to thirty-five years in denominational employment. Seventy percent were older than fifty, and as a group, they represented a broad geographical area—a total of twenty-five cities.

The researcher was concern about validity of the data. He expected sincere and balanced description of situation on the ground in response to the generalization and the theological problems. The researcher also expected the data or response from the respondent were reliable in the sense that the information they provided was dependable or consistent.

The responses were organized and sent to the Loma Linda Health Research Center in California for analysis. Thirty-one questionnaires were received, but thirty were analyzed by Loma Linda University Research center. Loma Linda organized the result into the following column valid, frequency and cumulative. Frequency column is the number of individuals or the position of the group receiving score in rank order. Cumulative frequency column represent the graphing of a cumulative distribution position of an individual in group. Valid represent how well or valid the questionnaire asked the right questions and how well individual gave a sincere and balanced description of the data source.

The data was analyzed using the following process. The data was entered in Microsoft Access 2000. Out of the thirty-one questionnaires, one had a different format. This survey was not entered.

The data was then imported from Access into Microsoft Excel 2000 and from Excel 2000 into SPSS (Statistical Package for Social Science) version 10.0.

Frequencies with histograms for each question were run. SPSS frequency tables and histograms were copied into Microsoft Word 2000. Finally, the data was compiled into a summary report with the most popular answers noted.

The final step involved developing practical training programs for improving community ministry in Michigan. The report was then finalized with a summary and conclusion.

Here is a summary report with the majority of the answers noted from the field questionnaire. The report also includes SPSS graphic frequency tables and histograms. The chapter concludes with a descriptive report of respondents' community service programs.

There are three areas the chapter will address: a brief biographical description of the respondents, the beliefs of the respondents, and a description of programs and services. The researcher used the data to rule out the generalization of Sahlin and Gavin.

Table 1
Gender

		Frequency	%	Valid %	Cumulative %
Valid	Male	21	70	70	70
	Female	9	30	30	100
	Total	30	100	100	

Table 2
Level of Education

		Frequency	%	Valid %	Cumulative %
Valid	High school	7	23.3	24.1	24.10
	One-year college	2	6.7	6.9	3.10
	Two-year college	2	6.7	6.9	37.9
	Three-year college	2	6.7	6.9	44.8
	Bachelor's degree	5	16.7	17.2	62.10
	Master's degree	10	33.3	34.5	96.60
	Doctorate	1	3.3	3.4	100
	Total	29	96.7	100	
	Missing System	1	3.3		
	Total	30	100.0		

Table 3
Employment of Respondents

		Frequency	%	Valid %	Cumulative %
Valid	0	1	3.3	3.3	3.3
	Pastor of urban, suburban, or rural church	18	60	60	63.3
	Community ministry director	6	20	20	83.3
	Unemployed	2	6.7	6.7	90.0
	Other	3	10	10	100.0
	Total	30	100	100	

Table 1 shows 70 percent of respondents were male, and 30 percent were female. Twenty-nine respondents provided their date of birth with 70 percent of the group being older than fifty.

Table 2 shows a range of educational levels reported in the group: 23.3 percent completed high school; 16.7 percent had bachelor's degrees (majors: education, civil engineering, mechanical engineering, theology, chemistry, and communication arts; minors: science, education, health, psychology, and language); 33.3 percent had master's degrees (majors: religion, reading education, theology, pastoral ministry, and elementary school administration); and 3.3 percent had doctorates in ministry.

Table 3 shows 60 percent of respondents indicated they were pastors of an urban, suburban, or rural church; 20 percent were community ministry directors; 6.7 percent were unemployed; and 10 percent did not indicate their profession.

The duration of service in their denomination varied, with 20 percent of respondents stating they had served for twenty-one to twenty-five years, while 16.7 percent had served for thirty-one to thirty-five years.

Table 4
Salvation is only about meeting people's spiritual needs.

		Frequency	%	Valid %	Cumulative %
Valid	0	1	3.3	3.3	3.3
	Don't know	1	3.3	3.3	6.7
	Strongly disagree	14	46.7	46.7	53.3
	Disagree	10	33.3	33.3	86.7
	Agree	4	13.3	13.3	100
	Total	30	100	100	

Table 5
The government, not the church, has the basic responsibility of caring for people who can't care for themselves.

		Frequency	%	Valid %	Cumulative %
Valid	0	1	3.3	3.3	3.3
	Don't know	1	3.3	3.3	6.7
	Strongly Disagree	6	20	20	26.7
	Disagree	13	43.3	43.3	70
	Agree	6	20	20	90
	Strongly agree	3	10	10	100
	Total	30	100	100	

Table 6
I am ministering when I help people establish
a relationship with God.

		Frequency	%	Valid %	Cumulative %
Valid	0	1	3.3	3.3	3.3
	Agree	4	13.3	13.3	16.7
	Strongly agree	25	83.3	83.3	100
	Total	30	100	100	

Table 7
My church has a community ministry leader.

		Frequency	%	Valid %	Cumulative %
Valid	0	2	6.6	6.7	6.7
	Don't know	1	3.3	3.3	10.0
	Disagree	3	10.0	10.0	10.0
	Agree	11	36.7	36.7	56.7
	Strongly agree	13	43.3	43.3	100
	Total	30	100	100	

Table 8
My church has a building for community ministry, programs, and services.

		Frequency	%	Valid %	Cumulative %
Valid	0	4	13.3	13.3	13.3
	Don't know	1	3.3	3.3	16.7
	Strongly disagree	3	10.0	10.0	26.7
	Disagree	6	20.0	20.0	46.7
	Agree	3	10.0	10.0	56.7
	Strongly agree	13	43.3	43.3	100
	Total	30	100	100	

Table 9
At present, my church is providing community ministry services.

		Frequency	%	Valid %	Cumulative %
Valid	0	3	10.0	10.0	10.0
	Disagree	2	6.7	6.7	16.7
	Agree	11	36.7	36.7	53.3
	Strongly agree	14	46.7	46.7	100.
	Total	30	100	100	

Table 10
I attend community ministry service annual training.

		Frequency	%	Valid %	Cumulative %
Valid	0	7	23.3	23.3	23.3
	Don't know	3	10.0	10.0	33.3
	Strongly Disagree	2	6.7	6.7	40.0
	Disagree	12	40.0	40.0	80.0
	Agree	4	13.3	13.3	93.3
	Strongly agree	2	6.7	6.7	100
	Total	30	100	100	

How does belief affect behavior of the respondents? Here, we measure behavior in terms of community ministry buildings', services, and leaders' training for pastors to support community social ministries. In Tables 4 and 5, we see high scores in the number of respondents who disagreed with the position that salvation is about spiritual needs and also about the opinion that the government is responsible. So, the issue of dualism is no problem for the respondents. How does this correspond to the generalization that there is a decline in number of community ministry buildings, centers, staff, programs, and services?

In Table 8, 53.3 percent of respondents said they have buildings for community ministry programs. In Table 9, 83.4 percent said that their churches are providing community ministry services. In Table 7, 80 percent of respondents either agreed or strongly agreed that their churches have community ministry leaders. In Table 10, when the respondents were asked about attending community ministry training annually, 20 percent said they attended community ministry training annually.

Field Faith-based social Programs and Services

The questionnaire asked respondents to write in their own words what programs and services they provide in the community. The following are responses transcribed directly from returned questionnaires. Each paragraph represents different response described by each respondent.

We have a separate building and help with clothing and help some with heating bills and rent in connection with our local capital area community services—the needs are screened carefully. Evangelistic meetings once a year (two baptized from our Community Services in 2001) represented at hair booth, cooking school, stress seminar, etc. Small-group Bible study weekly in home.

Our local church provides vegan cooking classes, stop smoking programs, basketball hoops at the edge of our parking lot, a pathfinder program, and an Adventist community services.

Our Community center works in close cooperation with all the other charity organizations in the community, such as Shelter House, Crisis Pregnancy Center, 1016 Treatment center (a halfway house for jail-released persons), Red Cross, Salvation Army, and so forth.

Our present need is to expand our floor space by a factor of four so our service can be expanded and our volunteers won't be climbing over each other. How important is this function of our church? If it weren't for the Community center in our community, they (the community) wouldn't know we were in town.

As our church is very small, my daughter and I run our church's clothes closet. We give free clothing and buy new if good used clothes are not available at the center. We also have some linen and literature available.

Community Services Center providing free clothing, bedding, towels. Work with other county service agencies—Health Department, schools, etc.

Our church provides clothing, food, personal items, and literature. We also help them in finding assistance in other areas.

Our area churches, schools, and individuals provide food and clothing for our center. We serve about fifty-eight families, two hundred individuals per month. We work well with other churches in the area. We have a great community.

We have an active community service center. We have a supply of good clothing at our center. We also pack many boxes a year to be shipped to others in need. We have some food available to give.

My church provides food and clothing to those in need. We are putting on a stop smoking seminar in the winter and also another for stress.

Gathered bags of food door-to-door for the needy, had a fair booth encouraging good health habits, prison ministry, youth funds for campers.

We distribute clothing when needed. Food program annually or when needed. Stress seminars for better emotional coping and planning parenting meeting.

People sleep on the porch of our church sometimes. This is way too much for a church to handle. Missions of food programs are one block away; we do not provide for the "neighborhood" community but rather those connected to our community of faith.

We host a Christian mental health group; we house some food in the church and give in emergencies. Our church community services director also works at a nonprofit community organization through which she also solves church problems.

Provide food. Involve soup kitchen, breathe-free smoking clinics, cooking schools and van ministry programs.

Currently, since we do not have a building, we are providing food items, emotional support, etc. We visit one-on-one, assisting where we deem needed and wanted. The members and pastor are involved in this ministry. We also provide Christmas baskets in addition to the year-round ministry.

Small church provides few community services. Mainly supplies food baskets sometimes.

The community is a major focus for our church. We have a community service program that is well known in our city. A pastor acts on a zone board that is of all denominations working together.

Our church participates in project Christmas each year, and we have a few staff that run the program. Ministry is training the members to use their God-given talents. It is not the pastor's job to micromanage every department the church offers. It is the pastor's job to hold the hands of the members so that they can fulfill their ministry.

I serve in leadership in an interdenominational community services program (RAM-LOVE). Our congregation will be more actively involved with C.S. [community services] when they have ministry space in their new church building.

We have a community services fund in the Three Rivers and Centerville churches. We supply food and clothes to people in need all year. At Christmas and Thanksgiving, we donate, through the Pathfinders, food baskets to the needy families. We work with the family independent agency in St. Joseph County. They give us names, and we follow up with assistance.

Whenever someone comes to our church with physical needs, we meet them. We have a food box right now to give to those with needs. I believe very strongly that physical needs should be met by the church, but with sharing the Christ as Lord and Savior.

Clothing center—opens at regular weekly times; referral to the other agencies, twenty-four-hour telephone access, smoking-cessation classes, healthful-cooking classes.

Clothing distributions, cooking schools, and food box distribution during the holidays.

A strong clothing, some food and furniture, family mentoring classes, and helpers to Saginaw Psychological services; Red Cross affiliation—our church is designated Red Cross emergency relief site; we cooperate with United Way and other agencies; various classes and seminars are sponsored in the name of our community services center.

It really helps in-gathering when the community sees an active church work through community services.

Food, clothing, prison ministry, supervision, and meals three weeks per year, meals for homeless on Sundays, help with gas for car, gas and electric occasionally, pack clothes for ADRA (Adventist Development and Relief Agency) counseling, in past used school for housing in summer months (have a house in community for that now).

My church operates a community service center, providing food and clothing. My other church provides money and food and clothing for the community without operating a center.

We help with food and clothing, help with some financial needs, feed homeless once a month, supervise homeless shelter two weeks a year, provide help for families of men in prison, do food baskets for holidays, provide a language school for non-English-speaking, provide place of worship for Spanish in community.

We have had great success with our C.S. [community services] program. I hope it will be running again in the spring (our church burnt down). We currently provide children's clothes to Central American orphanages and food to the local needy.

We have also helped a few people get some rotten teeth extracted for free! We meet needs for food and also financial needs as we find out about them—we have paid utility and rent bills at times, as we determined the need is legitimate.

We have had breathe-free plans to stop smoking, cooking schools, and health lectures. The health lectures (six to eight of them) run one night per week for six to eight weeks, with a vegetarian banquet at the close. We do this each year. We also hope to run a cooking school each year.

We must get back to opening our pastorate to more than just receiving a church program without feeling the felt needs of the community.

Support a van minority program, provide a monthly food bank program, fund community service fund to help persons in our community—emergency housing and emergency gas (voucher).

I have also included a description of the Detroit Yorba Food program.

The Detroit Yorba Project (housed at the Yorba Hotel, 4020 W. Lafayette, Detroit, Michigan 48209) is an emergency food program that provides hot meals to low-income residents of the Yorba Hotel, as well as to the homeless in the area. This project began in 1992.

Activities by the Yorba project include hot meals, a food pantry, bagged lunches, special foods for clients on medication, and an on-site food bank. The project leaders also work with human services providers as advocates on behalf of the people in the community.

During my visits to the Yorba Hotel Project, I saw several volunteers preparing full, quality, sit-down meals. The volunteers mingled with the guests and tried to make them feel welcome. Blessings on the food are part of the daily ritual.

An average of sixty to eighty hot meals served three days a week to the same number of people. Project volunteers also provide food baskets for those in need, a food bank for the community, cholesterol screening, and health-age appraisals.

In addition, project volunteers make phone calls to social workers, doctors, utility companies, and donors of supplies for food baskets. They also provide referral services to residents and give emotional support to those who have lost loved ones.

On-site hours for services were Sunday from 4:00 PM to 7:00 PM, Tuesday from 3:00 PM to 7:00 PM, and Thursday from 3:00 PM to 7:00 PM. Detroit/Metro Van Ministry.

The Detroit/Metro Van Ministries, started in 1985 by a group of laymen and pastors, was designed to reach out to minister to people in their own neighborhoods by addressing community health needs, winning the confidence of neighborhood residents, and then inviting them to learn more about their health needs. No fees have been charged for these services.

The purpose of Van Ministries is found in their mission statement: "It is our purpose to work in conjunction with the churches in the Detroit/Metro and Berrien County areas to develop Bible study interests, health seminar interests, and to improve community public relations. It is our goal to reach people where they are and to minister to their felt needs in order to address their spiritual needs."

The Detroit/Metro and Berrien County Van Ministries, in concert with area churches, have been serving their communities since the mid-1980s by developing interests for the various health seminars in the local churches.

The Van Ministries health screening shuttles drive to local neighborhoods, shopping centers, fairs, and businesses where church members and health professionals minister to the felt needs of that community. We trained van staff to conduct hypertension screening, health-age appraisal, lifestyle factor evaluations, and cholesterol screening.

Van staff members are trained to incorporate tactful spiritual questions in order to address the spiritual needs of those who come on the van, thus combining the medical and the evangelistic work in the context of the neighborhood situation where screened patrons live.

Those who come on the van are asked in a loving way if they would like to receive biblical guides on stress or Bible studies. Thirty-three percent of those who come on the van respond positively.

All types of interests are turned over to the local pastors or personal ministries leaders so that those who express an interest can be invited to various seminars or be followed up for Bible studies.

The area churches are currently establishing Bible schools for the overflow of those interested. Those who have lifestyle issues are given helpful literature to address their areas of need and/or are advised to see a doctor or a volunteer health provider in one of the area churches.

A pastor is currently working full-time with the Detroit-area van ministries to restructure and organize the work in the Detroit/Metro area. He speaks at local churches and conducts training sessions for those who would like to be a part of this community-based ministry.

Detroit/Metro Van Ministries is a Para-church district 12 ministry that is supported by the Michigan Conference, the Lake Union Conference, and by some private donations.

Van Ministries is audited annually by the General Conference auditing service and operates within the General Conference guidelines for van ministries. The van ministries use versa fund grants to buy needed literature, medical equipment, and medical supplies and to cover medical disposal costs.

A portion of the fund is needed for gasoline, oil, and maintenance on the shuttles. Van Ministries runs a year-round program budgeted for one year running from January through December. Every year it turns over thousands of names for Bible studies and for health programs to the local churches. The maximum number of persons this project can serve, if funded, is about thirteen thousand to fifteen thousand; the number of persons currently being served is 10,400.

The project depends on volunteers from Seventh-day Adventist churches and the community to fill job vacancies. Volunteers are needed to prepare food, staff the mobile shuttle, and follow up the needs of residents that use the service. The project also works with pastors in the local community and their members to access the needs of residents in the area.

The goal of the Mobile Health Shuttle is to reach poor families where they are and provide them with free health screening. The Mobile Shuttle works in conjunction with local area health institutions to improve the health of the population living in the city. It also aims to reach families living below the poverty line to minister to their physical needs.

The Mobile Health Shuttle serves low-income families in an attempt to change their health risk behaviors. It provides assistance to poor families to improve their diet by eating less fat, eliminating excess cholesterol from their foods, etc.

Van Ministries provides information on why smoking is bad for one's health and also provides support groups. Staff educate community populations on alcohol abuse and its effects.

The following list conveys the many tasks undertaken by the van ministries:

- Promote the concepts of faith-based ministries.
- Organize groups to study the issue.
- Recruit participants or staff.
- Develop group programs, mission statements, goals, objectives, and activities.
- Appoint a board.
- Interface with health-related and poverty agencies for clients.
- Develop a grant proposal.
- Keep records of clients.

Programs and Social Entrepreneurship

The church community services (ACS) programs vary from place to place based on local need. Centers are operated in about five hundred cities and towns across the United States, Canada, and Bermuda. In thousands of other locations, ACS projects work out of church basements and borrowed facilities. The work of a community services volunteer might include any of the following programs:

Adopt a grandparent	Advocacy Programs	Bible Study Group
Family Camping	Family Life Workshop	First Aid Class
Intake desk	Job-finding service	Legal aid
Adoption services	Alcohol Programs	Big Brother/Big Sister
Family Counseling	Field Trips	Follow up Contact
Interagency liaison	Job training program	Literacy tutoring
ADRA Volunteering	Baby Care Classes	Blind Camp
Family Finance Center	Financial Counseling	Food Bank/Food Pantry
Interviewing clients	Layettes	Literature rack
Blind Services	Community Surveys	Senior citizens group

Food Distribution	Grief recovery seminar	Door-to-Door Contacts
Marriage seminar	Preparing for baby classes	Home nursing classes
Board Member	Cooking School	Sewing class
Foster Childcare	Handicapped services	Drug Abuse Detox
Meals on Wheels	Prison ministry	Immigration program
Branch Sabbath School	Counseling Service	Shoes for Little Shavers
Foster Grand parenting	Health appraisals	Drug Abuse Rehabilitation
Migrant ministry	Public relations	Information and referral services
Camping for Children	Craft Classes	Smoking cessation program
Free clinic	Health education	Families of Prisoners
Operation Overcoat	Receptionist	Inner-city programs
Children's Story Hour	Deaf Services	Soup kitchen
Fund-raising	Health screening	Stress seminar
Operation Paintbrush	Refugee ministry	Suicide prevention
Clothing/Bedding Program	Disaster Relief	Support groups
Furniture program	Home nursing	Tax assistance
Parenting seminar	Runaway shelter	Telephone friend program
Community Cupboard	Divorce Recovery Seminar	Transients' aid
Craftsmanship	Homeless shelter	Transportation assistance
Pathfinder club	Self-help groups	Tutoring
Van ministry	Domestic Violence	Vacation Bible school

Videos for education	Homemaker services	Visiting the sick
Visiting the aged	Visiting the sick	Weight control program

Participants in the study were unified in the church theological support for community social ministry. An appeal for training in community social ministry reverberated among the participants. The knowledge and skills for community social ministry are in great demand.

The task now is developing a theological support for socioeconomic development and social entrepreneurship, with intent of raising awareness for human identity and dignity to subdue and have dominion or control over the resources of the earth. It is important to attempt to develop a theological foundation because of the split over the topic. The topic is quiet a sensitive subject that not many willing theologians would like to touch because of past experience of the failure of the social gospel and liberation theology attempts to have a broad support. It is unacceptable to ignore the subject because of the trend and challenges of socioeconomic problems and it connection to human identity, dignity and dominion over the earth and it resources for sustainable existential development. The reason is understood, because one does not want to be caught in the crossfire. And what if you are wrong and your theology is called into question like the liberation theology?

If the solution lies in biblical support, then it has to be neutral and more in support of the God of creation and all that are created, including man's responsibility. In other words, can we find a link between God or divinity and the material world to be the basis of faith-based community social ministry?

Chapter Eight

Insight for Faith-based Socioeconomic Development

The field study shows that the respondents support church involvement in faith-based socioeconomic and social entrepreneurship. Therefore, developing a theoretical foundation to support a faith-based development was the next step of the researcher. He completed this task in chapter eight and nine.

The researcher accomplished this by creating a theological and biblical foundation using Genesis 1–3 to develop a foundation for faith-based socioeconomic development. The same chapters have been used by the church for centuries to develop a foundation for Christian spiritual theology, mission, and ministry, giving rise to worship and both public and personal evangelism.

The justification for developing foundation for socioeconomic development and social entrepreneurship cannot be over emphasized. The economic realities of the poor and middle class that continue to affect individuals and families and in turn causing massive lay-off, poor economic growth, decline in tax revenue, weaken consumer spending and demand for raw materials, human resources, production by manufacturer and demand by consumer.

All indication is showing us the sign that they way man has used natural resources and human resources for production, services and consumption has not been very effective. We have for centuries associated prosperity and economic growth to job security, demand in products, cash flows and consumer confidence. Others have use natural and human resources to create class of the developed and developing or the richest and the poorest.

It seems that we have to change course and direction and perhaps consider economic growth as the ability of all to create and have access to material and human resources when they needed it at all time. Present economy has failed for generations to achieve that instead have created a system of economy that thrive on debt, wages, rich and poor. The present economy is only working well for the rich that have the contact and pool of funds natural and human resources for wealth and gain. This explains why some will want to buy and stored all the natural resources for control and wealth creation than for access to all.

Therefore, finding an approach that will increase individual awareness of the creator, the relationship between the creator and created resources, and human responsibility towards God, the earth and it natural resources is urgently needed to establish human dominion for socioeconomic development and entrepreneurship among individuals or nations that have failed to invest in self and the natural resources of the earth for sustainable living.

Perhaps, we could broaden the scope of Christian theology, training, mission and ministry in modern time to include socioeconomic and social entrepreneurship programs. Whether you serve as a social worker, business service provider, medical professional, environmentalist, food service worker, family service worker, or political service worker, Genesis has some ideas or starting points for your work.

Theology and mission can no longer be limited to spiritual problems and issues but should also embrace the total creative sovereignty of God that includes man in the image and likeness of God and man's dominion over the material world and material resources.

Material resources cannot be created or added to. The church has a responsibility not only to focus on death, dying, and future resurrection but to also focus on life in the present world designed by God with existential resources to sustain life. There are good reason and logic why a divine spiritual being created the material world and its resources before he created mankind. It seems the material world was a top priority in the order of creation.

The real situation in the world is material resources are on the decline, and the demand for material resources will continue its upward trend. Also, regions or countries where material resources are in abundance still lack the knowledge and skills required to develop the resources, because education is not linked to the environment or resources.

The church and social services may be tempted to preach and teach about God or higher power while ignoring to teach and preach about God and the created resources entrusted to human dominion. I have heard countless time theologians have attempted to convince me sin caused man to lose his dominion completely over the earth and it material resources therefore, we should leave material resources out of the theology and training of the church. Also, I have seen the programs and services of social services dispensed without mention of existential resources and human dominion and image.

Therefore, the drive and need for material resources for survival will continue to be a leading cause of social crisis, economic collapse, and political and economic instability in the so-called, stereotyped developing and developed world. As a result, the demand for socioeconomic programs and social services to substitute normal life, crisis services, and goods will continue to increase as more and more individuals have less and less access to natural existence resources. Our world has been poorly designed with the best of intention to cut off masses from vital existential resources.

Therefore, the poor will continue to experience generational dependence on the rich in the developed and developing nation with access to natural existence resources and the rich will continue to exploit the poor for labor, low wages and demand for more money for payment of goods and services induce by poor credit score charges designed to punish unworthy credit payment behavior but at the same time rewarding and enriching the wealthy until responsible steps are taken to educate both rich and poor about their true identities and shared dominion.

Therefore, the need for a theological message that addresses man's responsibility toward material resources is urgent, because we cannot continue the old ways of talking about the Creator and neglect to talk about our responsibility toward created things. Also, we can not continue to provide social services to the poor while failing to teach and educate the poor about their self-worth created in the image and likeness of God to have dominion over their environment lacking in the life of the poor.

The church has a responsibility to be actively involved in educating individuals and leaders to invest in and access vital existential resources. Any attempt to commercialize and politicize any of these assets for the wealth of a few may trigger universal socioeconomic upheaval and crisis.

Moral asset is the key that holds everything. A decline in a moral asset may trigger unforeseeable consequences. Also, failure to integrate and emphasize or develop these assets for holistic human development may cause an unnecessary holistic imbalance and socioeconomic stagnation that exist among the poor. It is clear from the biblical example of the life of Adam and Eve that abundance of natural resources and potential for socioeconomic development may be present but if the individuals with dominion over the earth have moral problems and challenges like in the case of Adam and Eve as we will see in chapter ten development and prosperity will stifle. Modern man continues to suffer similar faith of Adam and Eve until succeeding generation bridge the gap between moral development and dominion as necessary ingredient or pepper and salt relationship for success. But success, depending on what that is and the variables that determine success, happens when there is full awareness and understanding of identity and the responsibility associated with human identity in a social context and service delivery system.

Social ministry in this study means a combination of effort and action to achieve social justice, as well as to provide needed social services[67] to those in need. Miles notes: "Social ministry is feeding the hungry, giving drink to the thirsty, welcoming strangers, clothing the naked, and visiting the sick and the prisoners."[68]

According to Garland, Christian social ministry refers to activities carried out by redeemed individuals called by God to proclaim the good news, to minister to the needy, and to seek justice for all.[69] Garland adds that providing human service is vital only as it is integrated into the overall purpose of the church.[70]

Gorrell states: "We have seen that the crisis of society is also the crisis of the church." [71] Few Christian leaders share this position. Literature generally points out that the Christian churches, and specifically the church that is the center of the study, are divided on the response.

Bennett states that "human needs and social problems can no longer be relegated to an optional appendix which Christians can choose to ignore."[72] Because the Christian church can no longer ignore this problem. The Church must find a biblical insight justifying community social ministry.

Nicholls states: "The task before the Christian church is systematic theology, the intellectual formulation of the faith of Christian needs to be done again in every age, and more frequently as the pace of change accelerates."[73]

Smith looks at the role of the church in mission and pastoral ministry from a holistic view and declares that the Christian church has a responsibility to provide not only spiritual services and programs for its members but also to provide services and programs for a better quality life.[74]

Smith adds that the church on earth has the potential to help revamp low-income areas of North America. Smith maintains that the church is ministering when it feeds, counsels, and houses people.[75]

Caleb Rosado seems to combine the ministry of preaching with the role of the church in society. In order to preach, one must fully understand the content of the Gospel and also develop a clear understanding of the people to whom the Gospel will be given in society.[76]

Edgar J. Ellison underscores the importance of the person in the social environment and states that the key problem and challenge to Christian ministry and pastoral care in this decade will be rooted in economics.[77] Ellison wrote that the former president of Asbury Theological Seminary has said that economics may be the most significant social issue for the church in this modern age of information.[78]

Donald Gorrell expands the scope of Christian mission and ministry by drawing attention to society in general. He states that we have seen that the crisis of society is also the crisis of the church.[79]

If this argument is true, we must find a biblical support for faith-based social ministry. However, the danger any researcher confronts today as he attempts to develop scriptural support for community social ministry is by no means more menacing than the danger of disagreeing with the question of whether Christian mission and ministry is about humanity's spirituality or materialism or both.

John Bennett drives home the question that confronts any Christian researcher attempting to find scriptural support for a topic that is not present in scripture. Are social problems of people the problem of the Gospel? [80]

Chapter Nine

Genesian Foundation for Socioeconomic Development

Many of the problems we have today in the material world like poverty may be self inflicted. Religion has excluded it self voluntarily from the role and place it should represent in the material world created by God and given to human beings to subdue the earth and it resources and create dominion for all. Also, the concept dominion to govern, rule etc has been limited in some part the world only to control of people than the earth and it resources. Religious leaders are not involving in educating their youths and family about the creator and created things and their responsibility to develop the earth and it resources. A lot of religious emphasis has been place on the here after and life and death than emphasis on present life, education and skills on how to subdue the earth and it resources and have domino consistent with biblical demands. Some religion has not only shifted emphasis on the here and after but also engaged in practices that cause death and reward war and violence.

While religion has abstained from it role representing God on earth and the interest of God towards human being living on earth as the image and likeness of God subduing the earth and it resources, political leadership on the other hand has moved in the direction of dominion and control of people than development of human and natural resources living human resources and natural resources to business leaders that exploit human and material resources not for education, training, research, job creation, goods and services and shared benefit for all but for themselves. Reversing this poor thinking and behavior that has been standing in the way of fighting poverty and spread of wealth and dominion for all is fundamental for getting out of poverty and growing prosperous communities and people.

It all depends how we look at creation and the fall of man and the crisis that came out of the fall. The data from the field study is consistent with the fact that respondent overwhelmingly agreed and see a role the church and society can play in socioeconomic development and social entrepreneurship. The data also points to the need for training church members and leaders in this line of profession. It is possible training will increase awareness and responsibility towards God and towards created things. Also, the tension does not go away by the result of the study. There is still a need as you can see to develop a theology in support for faith-based socioeconomic development and social entrepreneurship to enhance the awareness of the poor about God and their dominion responsibility towards created existential resources or CER.

This need has led the researcher to attempt for the first time to utilize a new approach for understanding and practice of socioeconomic development and social entrepreneurship that resonate with biblical principles and dominion. This may become useful in cities and parts of the world were the poor acknowledge the presence of God but lacked awareness of their divine identity, settled for systems designed to undermine the image of man thus destroying individual commitment to development and dominion.

We want to have a world where the talk is not centered only on God but what he has made us to become and what he has delegated us to do, to have dominion. If all individuals, families and nations are doing their part there is something for everyone to invest, develop, and benefit from while staying connected with God and created things.

How did God meet human physical needs? Did God pay attention to human physical needs? God had a holistic plan in place before the first human beings were created.

Genesis 1–3, used by Christian churches for centuries to teach about mans disobedience, punishment of death and life through Jesus Christ also has the key for the foundation of human socioeconomic development and social entrepreneurship. hardly mentioned in theological trainings, bible study, family circles, political circles, social services and business circles. Therefore, understanding the relationship between the creator and the created things is fundamental in any development. The book of Genesis chapter 1-2 is clear that God created matter for human needs.

The book of Genesis is the foundation of human identity, spirituality, socioeconomic development principles, and human problems and crisis that continue to plague succeeding generation. Genesis chapter 1-3 holds the key to understanding who we are as humans created in the image and likeness of God to have dominion over the earth we have been created to govern. The book also holds the list of resources needed for economic and social entrepreneurship, including solar energy, hydropower, dairy products, minerals, land and timber, reproduction issues, health issues, family issues, nutrition, etc.

Genesis sets three levels of relationships necessary for socioeconomic development: first, God or higher power; second, man; and third, natural resources. A balanced understanding of relationship in the first two chapters of Genesis is the door out of poverty among the poor and the developing nations.

In Genesis chapter 1, 2 and 3 is the key to all human relationships, progress, and development. Therefore, it is safe to start developing the foundation for faith-based socioeconomic development and social programs by using the first three chapters of the book of Genesis. The researcher decided to start laying the principal foundation for faith-based socioeconomic development or entrepreneurship by devoting discussion to Genesis 1–3.

What does Genesis say about human needs and the material world? This section assesses human needs both before and after the fall of man.

Genesis is the first book of the Bible, and in Jewish tradition, the book was named from its first word *bereshith* (in the beginning).[81] The name *Genesis*, which means *beginning*, was derived from the Septuagint (Greek Bible) and is found also in the Latin tradition (Liber Genesis).[82]

Genesis contains the world's only authentic written record of creation and the history of the antediluvian world. It also gives the only reliable account of the deluge.[83]

Harris believes the book contains the record of sacred history from the first day of the creation week to the death of Joseph in Egypt.[84]

Hiseberger describes what sets Genesis 1–11 apart: the recounting of the origin of the world and of man (primeval history).[85]

Other relevant information found in Genesis includes many religious teachings: the pre-existence and transcendence of God, his wisdom and goodness, his power through which all things were made and on which they all depend, and the special creation of man in God's image and likeness.

The material environment of man was central to Divine Creation. Man cannot experience the fullness of God's creative acts if he is denied access to, or cannot afford to bring into his possession, supplies or resources for his survival. This is not to suggest that is the total responsibility of the church to provide man's natural resources.

However, the church, by virtue of its calling to represent God on earth, has an obligation to encourage and support man in his efforts to bring in available resources necessary for holistic balance. Therefore, success of faith-based social work will depend on how faith-based social workers use integrated knowledge to create or improve the lives of people. The Genesian approach is the safest and most effective way to do this. The Genesian approach was developed by the researcher upon discovering the three areas of relationship for holistic development found in Genesis 1–3.

Relationship and Development
Genesis 1 opens with a statement in recognition of God as the creator of the world, it resources including man. The book of Genesis holds the key to understanding humans' relationship with God or higher power, between the sexes, and with the material environment. All three are essential for faith-based socioeconomic development.

Genesis seems to hold the key to a successful holistic relationship and development. Individual will have to make honest inventory about were in the relationship they are involving and making progress and where they have neglected and need to be involve. Holistic socioeconomic development is dependent on three levels of relationships:

1. A relationship **with God**, who created mankind as living beings in his image and likeness (Gen. 2:7, 8, 18, 28 and Gen. 2:16–17) whose act and behavior exhibited a blue print for socioeconomic development and social entrepreneurship.

2. Relationship between **male and female** (Gen. 2: 18, 21–24) and the reproduction of human resources to interact with created existential resources. Human relationship or couple relationship was created by God for specific responsibilities, which Adam by himself could not have performed alone even when it appeared and presented he would have until he was told "it is not good for man to live alone". The female being was created with equal divine nature as the image and likeness of God, with equal responsibilities to accomplish the following: subdue the earth and it resources, have domino, re-produce or responsible to increase in numbers, rule over the fish of the sea, birds, every living creature, responsible for the plants, food yielding seeds, work and care for their environment, rest or worship and be obedient or take responsibility for respect the rights of others property (Genesis 2:28; 1:28-31 and Gen 2:15-17). These responsibilities formed the early beginning of human relationship or couple relationship. It is fair to say that socioeconomic development thrives in a relationship context than when it is not. Therefore, people exist as

couple with well defined responsibilities so that no one will exploit the other for personal gain other than collective responsibilities. If relationships are develop with these responsibilities in focus, socioeconomic development is bound to occur in a meaningful ways because there are variety of things to do in a relationship than to limit oneself to just one responsibility and activity. Therefore, the following constituents God, human identity, relationship and human responsibilities should be key emphasis in socioeconomic development and entrepreneurship. There lot of things to do in a relationship than being stocked, ran out of ideas and activities as it is in some relationship. Relationship and family context offers the best venue for effective socioeconomic development and entrepreneurship. Our identity, relationships with God, couple, family and the material world should help guide our behavior, religious beliefs and devotion and also our career choices and socioeconomic preferences.

3. A relationship with **created things** (Gen. 1: 28) man was created with dominion over the earth and it resources. Individual has to be taught the value of socioeconomic relationship and development. Each of the three areas is necessary for holistic development and success.

How to articulate and translate the three levels of relationship into socioeconomic and social entrepreneurship will be the challenge for the poor and the church in the 21st century.

Faith-based socioeconomic development does not seek to engage in the debate for and against. However, faith-based socioeconomic development practitioners will work to make the lives of people better by refocusing attention on relationships with the Creator, between the sexes, and with created things. God is the center of everything. God is the creator.

Also, helping individuals develop a relationship with God must focus on the attributes of God as the divine resource provider with special moral attributes for socioeconomic development that include goodness, impartiality, love, mercy, long-suffering, justice, holiness, and truth. Faith-based social workers and socioeconomic developers can use these attributes and knowledge to enrich their moral insight and practices as socioeconomic providers.

Created Existential Resources (CER)

Table 11 and 12 shows how God met basic human needs. God created existential resources for human access, development, activities and use. Material resources or human resources were never used to measure the difference between the poor and rich. What was important was that God wanted to make sure Adam and Eve had access to vital existence resources as we see in table 11.

Natural resources is essential components of human's divine created environment. Individuals and nations that have tapped into their natural resources have done far better than individuals and nations that have not or do very little to invest and convert their CER for existential necessities, commerce, and wealth development. Let us look at what God created and its implication for faith-based social work.

Heaven: The Bible teaches that the heavens declare the glory of God (Ps. 19:1). Genesis 1:7 describes how Heaven was created. God made the sky, or heaven, by word of mouth. There is water above the sky and below the sky. The heavens also represent the place or realm in which the sun, moon, and stars are positioned. The richness of the concept of heaven, whether it is a reference to the sky or the abode of God, represents the ideal goal for mankind.

Therefore, helping people attain and experience a foretaste of what represents their heaven is the key to faith-based programs. People in crisis seek help because they want to return to their stable environment. They are looking for supporting order to experience peace and stability. The concept of heaven has some positive characteristics in the minds of people, which include bliss, joy, rest, peace, glory, reward, inheritance, and service.

Earth: The dry land with many laden gifts and natural treasures is the environment of man, animal, and all other forms of life. It is a rich subject. The Earth is made of matter. Matter is anything that occupies space and has weight. The basic states of matter include a solid phase, a liquid phase, and a gaseous phase.

The Earth has motion, fluid, heat, sound, light, electricity, magnetism, relativity, atomic structures, particles, and dust; astrophysics contains tremendous possibilities for all forms of energy if annexed appropriately and effectively.

Physics is a science constructed in human terms to help us understand the physical structure of the Earth. Biology, the study of life forms, is useful in helping us understand forms of life, man, and plants in the evolutionary context of adaption and the interaction between organisms in their environments.

Faith in a spiritual being that created the world should include an integrated study of God (spirituality), the heavens (astronomy), and earth (earth sciences, physics, chemistry, biology, etc.). Therefore, faith-based social work should integrate God, heaven, and earth in direct practice. Faith-based social work must be a consistent effort to improve an individual's knowledge not only about God, but also about things he created, including the heavens and the earth.

The poorer nations of the world, the so-called third-world countries, or developing countries, sit on vast wealth for industry and commerce. These nations lack knowledge and technical skills necessary to convert natural resources into marketable goods and services for distribution, exchange and use for survival.

When an individual or nation fails to integrate God, heaven, and earth in the spiritual and daily experience, lack of progress is experienced. The created things offer wonderful opportunities for research, development, manufacturing, and services for exchange, financial incentives and job creation. Also, the created things, both living and nonliving, are the best way to learn about God-created wisdom.

Experience warned of the consequences of introducing God to individuals while ignoring the other object of God's creation (heaven and earth). In fact, this may be one of the leading causes of poverty, because individuals have not been exposed and taught responsibility toward the Creator and created things. In other words, they have been taught to know God, love him, and serve him without being committed to the things he created.

Imagine the poor and poorer nations tapping into their natural resources for holistic development, industrial development, and commerce. The result will be job creation, social development, economic development, and holistic prosperity, which is absent at present in many of the developing countries. Therefore, the church has a role to teach not only about God but about man's creative responsibility toward heaven and the resources of the earth.

Faith-based social workers should teach about the relationship between God (spirituality), the heavens, and the earth. You cannot love God and ignore the heavens and the earth. It is like sharing a house with a friend but failing to care for his house. Faith-based social work is about encouraging individuals, families, churches, and world governments to integrate their love for God with the objects of God's creative power (the heavens and the earth) for holistic development.

Genesis describes the different elements that constitute man's first natural environment and the natural resources that were created. Created existential resources (CER) are the key to human development and dominion. CER are the basic building blocks for all human needs and socioeconomic and industrial development. The less an individual has access to resources, the more vulnerable he becomes and the higher the risk of poverty. This is why all policies must be consistent to support dominion.

What we know from scripture is that man was originally a living being created in the image and likeness of God to have dominion over the resources and the earth. There are many variant interpretations about what has happened to the image man as he was created with resources to rule over. Let us review a list of the resources (CER) we have compiled from Genesis 1–3.

This list holds the key to all socioeconomic developments. What resources are you involved with now, should have been involved with, or will be involved with? What will it take to train you with the skills and knowledge to have dominion over any of these resources? What will you have to do now to get, involve, or create investment opportunities, jobs, and income? Is your government investing in any of these areas or sectors? As a nation or individual, do you spend a lot of money buying natural resources and supplying, refining, or converting natural resources into goods and services?

Natural resources are an excellent opportunities for job creation, education, research, investment, six-day of labor, gainful employment and sharing. But historical observation shows natural resources have been abuse. A faulty understanding of natural resources have led to the wide spread practice of using natural resources as a means of money making enterprise to an extent that it has completely limits it purpose as existential resources. Natural resources are the building blocks of human survival, manufacturing of product, distribution of goods and services. There are nation whose use of natural resources is selling and at the same time can not afford to buy the goods made from the resources they sold.

Also, natural resources have been used for political advantages as nations wage war or destabilize other nations for supply. We have also seen how individuals have been used to produce goods and services but on less and less pay while the owners rewarded themselves with fat checks. We have seen how private political groups have taking over a nation natural resource for political use than for socioeconomic development of a nation. This abuse of converting national resources into private use has left many individuals at risk for poverty.

There is urgent need to re-evaluate our understanding of the use of natural resources, knowledge, skills and services developed around natural resources. One of the questions that will confront succeeding generation is who should be responsible for the knowledge, skills and investment required for developing natural resources to make them available to all? Should we encourage small business to have complete control, private political groups or the government? If we say the government or small business what percentage of control should each have and how will the population have access and not being hit by too higher a cost that will live many going with out CER? How should we prevent abuse of human and natural resources?

The other issue is the need for educating individuals and families about natural resources and the opportunities to convert each resource through education, skills training, job creation, investment and commerce. It is the fact of life that in many poor cities and towns there is poor educational system and infrastructure for socioeconomic development in place. Resources from land and sea will continue to offer the greatest resources for socio economic development than we have come to appreciate. There are many subjects about natural resources that could be taught to families because every goods and products on the shelves or stores have evolved from natural resources.

Human beings have relied and will continue to rely on natural resources for industry, production, commerce, research, programs and services. Here is a list of natural resources form Genesis 1-2 in table 11. The list is the core of resources the researcher has identified from Genesis chapter one and two. Also, after this list the researcher has added the world list of natural resources as we see them today in table 12.

Table 11

Created Existential resources (CER)	Bible reference
Earth and land	Genesis 1:10
Trees and woods	Genesis 2: 9
Food: plants, seeds, and herbs	Genesis 1:11; 12, 29
Fruits and vegetables	Genesis 1: 11
Solar and lunar energy	Genesis 1:16–18
Birds	Genesis 1:20
Sea: minerals/oil	Genesis 1:10
Sea: animals and food	Genesis 1:21
Fish	Psalms 8:8
Land animals and cattle	Genesis1:24–25
Creeping things	
Sheep and oxen	Psalms 8:6
Rivers: hydro-energy	Genesis 2:10–14
Mineral resources: gold and precious metals	Genesis 2:11

Table 12

Natural resources in Africa, Europe and USA

The list below gives us some idea of natural resources that has been discovered by man in the earth. As you look at the list you will come to appreciate fact that God created the earth with abundant natural resources for human socioeconomic development. God was not only a creator to love and serve but he created resources for human dominion. Man use of resources will be influenced by individual understanding of creation, human identity and dominion over the earth all three occurring within the context of created relationship. Sad to say the world has not fully comprehend the relationship and thus have conduct or use natural resources for capital interest, ego recognition, stereotypes classification of the rich and poor and self interest. Until this misunderstanding is corrected we will continue to see the gap between access and non access, exploitation, ego recognition, stereotypes and poverty continues to rise. Also, nations will continue to exploit other nations with abundant of resources but have no knowledge, skills, technical and infrastructure in place to develop their natural resources. Meaningful exchange of natural resources should include education, skills, investment and infrastructure development provided to nations with no knowledge, skills, investment and infrastructure to exercise dominion over their resources.

The poor are in dire needs of increasing their awareness of identity and dominion in the world and over the resources in their environment. Future faith-based socioeconomic development and social entrepreneurship should focus on identity development, dominion development and investment for all than for few as it has been for decades. Individuals should travel to any part of the earth and be able to access resources for existential living because the resources of the world were created to benefit all. Let us take a look at natural resources that has been discovered in countries around the world.

Cote d'Ivoire petroleum, natural gas, diamonds, manganese, iron ore, cobalt, bauxite, copper, gold, nickel, tantalum, silica sand, clay, cocoa beans, coffee, palm oil, hydropower

China coal, iron ore, petroleum, natural gas, mercury, tin, tungsten, antimony, manganese, molybdenum, vanadium, magnetite, aluminum, lead, zinc, uranium, hydropower potential (world's largest)

Egypt petroleum, natural gas, iron ore, phosphates, manganese, limestone, gypsum, talc, asbestos, lead, zinc

France metropolitan France: coal, iron ore, bauxite, zinc, uranium, antimony, arsenic, potash, feldspar, fluorspar, gypsum, timber, fish

Ghana gold, timber, industrial diamonds, bauxite, manganese, fish, rubber, hydropower, petroleum, silver, salt, limestone

Kenya limestone, soda ash, salt, gemstones, fluorspar, zinc, diatomite, gypsum, wildlife, hydropower

Nigeria natural gas, petroleum, tin, iron ore, coal, limestone, niobium, lead, zinc, arable land

South Africa gold, chromium, antimony, coal, iron ore, manganese, nickel, phosphates, tin, uranium, gem diamonds, platinum, copper, vanadium, salt, natural gas

Sierra Leone diamonds, titanium ore, bauxite, iron ore, gold, chromite

United States coal, copper, lead, molybdenum, phosphates, uranium, bauxite, gold, iron, mercury, nickel, potash, silver, tungsten, zinc, petroleum, natural gas, timber **note:** the US has the world's largest coal reserves with 491 billion short tons accounting for 27% of the world's total

United Kingdom coal, petroleum, natural gas, iron ore, lead, zinc, gold, tin, limestone, salt, clay, chalk, gypsum, potash, silica sand, slate, arable land

Some of the countries in the list have developed some knowledge, skills, investment and structure for socioeconomic development and dominion over the earth and it resources but others have not till now. This is true of the poor and rich in Detroit, Michigan and many cities in the USA. How do we change that so that everyone is exercising dominion and benefitting? Answer to this question will be the test of genuine socioeconomic development and social entrepreneurship in the twenty-first century.

As long as many of the poor in the developed and developing nations continue to drift away from CER or failed to convert their resources into programs, goods and services, the wide gap that now exist between the rich and the poor and the middle and the upper class will continue to grow instead of diminishing fostering dependence, poor socioeconomic and holistic development in the developed and developing nations.

The problem in modern system of economic practice and policies is the poor and middle class are used as human resources to create wealth for few families in control of CER. Also, many countries in the developing nations are not getting equal benefit for their natural resources because, their leaders continue to operate ancient economic satellite station practices giving land out with natural resources for few amount excluding the value of the mineral in the land. Land and mineral resources are the wealth of a nation and should not be treated slightly or dismissed while people walk away with the wealth from the mineral resources because he is not required to pay taxes on the mineral but only on the land use. If we continue to keep this old practices the poor will be come poorer while rich families operating companies walk away with great wealth that should have been shared from both use of the land and value of the mineral wealth in the land. The church must engage individuals and families to participate line by line in developing created existential resources for human wellbeing.

The church has a big role to play because it claims that it is the representative of God on earth. The church can create a theology of identity and dominion as it has in theology of God for educating individuals and families about the relationship between the creator, man as the image and likeness of God and dominion for socioeconomic development and entrepreneurship in the twenty-first century. It is unacceptable for individuals and families to live without access to natural resources for development, job creation, programs and services to improve life in all parts of the world.

How can the church encourage families, private and national sectors to exercise dominion over resources entrusted in their care and region? What are the implications if the public or private sector has been lagging to invest in the education and infrastructure for socioeconomic development? Table 13 below gives us an idea of the social structures that should be in place for socioeconomic development. Table 14 is a list of moral structures that should be in place for equal benefit of socioeconomic development, social entrepreneurship and dominion.

Table 13

Human resources and Social Structure	Bible reference
Man: male	Genesis 1:26–27
Woman: female, helper	Genesis 2:23
Human union: male and female	Genesis 2:18, 24
Reproductive abilities and care	Genesis 2:28
Man's position and dominion	Genesis 2:28
Man's task: reproduce and control resources	Genesis 2:28
Tend & Keep	Genesis 2:15
Man's environment: garden	Genesis 2:8

Table 14

Moral Structure	Bible reference
Tree of Life	Genesis 2:9
Tree of Knowledge of Good and Evil	Genesis 2:9
What is allowed	Genesis 2:16
What is not allowed, punishment	Genesis 2:17
Spiritual and moral development	Genesis 2: 7, 9
Stewardship	Genesis 1:28: 2:15

The interplay and interaction of man's image and abilities with the natural environment and created existential resources (CER) is the foundation for socioeconomic development.

The theory is clear: the greater the distance between a man and the CER and any problem or poor development in any area of the structures is a prediction for poverty. The risk can be higher as we assess where each individual, families or nations stands. Also, if theology or mission of the church continues to over look each area of the structures by lack of training or emphasis situation for the poor will not improve. Also, if government programs failed to integrate each element in socioeconomic situation will continue as is and the life of the poor will not improve.

The poor in Detroit or any other part of the world share certain problems in common: lack of insight about identity, access to existential resources and poor dominion development over the earth.

Natural resources will continue to dominate man's thoughts, interests, and focus. Early education, research and training should be tied to the development of natural resources, crisis services, investment opportunities, development, and job creation.

Food

John Leighly states that man was made with his food plants "forming" a biological complex in which mankind and their food plants developed.[86]

George Berry explains the process that made the Lord grow every tree that is pleasant to his sight for food (Gen. 2:9).[87] Terry Armstrong interpreted the word *grow* to mean cause to grow, to sprout, or to be desirable for food[88]—other words similar to *food* include tree, herbs, and green.

Freeman thinks that food has become part of man's survival needs and must be fulfilled at some upper level before other, higher-order needs are activated.[89] Food is needed as a fuel for the maintenance of the energy-requiring processes that sustain life.[90]

New evidence in the field of nutrition shows every individual needs food to produce energy. Energy is required for maintaining the psychochemical environment of an intact animal, the so-called internal milieu, and for sustaining the electro-technical activities that define the organism.[91] Evidence shows that food is necessary for human growth.

Ziegler and Filer cite Paul George's study of children not only in his hometown of Philadelphia, but also in many parts of the world, especially

Indonesia. George's research shows childhood malnutrition would become apparent if the individual lived long enough.[92]

Martin Linder identified the three basic uses of energy:

Basal metabolism: This is the metabolic activity required for the basic maintenance of body life and function. Basal means levels of oxygen consumption of a person awake but at complete rest in a neutral, warm environment after fasting overnight.[93]

Physical activity: The need for energy increases each time we engage in physical exercise.[94.]

Specific dynamic: This is the energy needed for staying and keeping warm. This energy comes from food.[95] Many of the developing nations need assistance, knowledge and skills to process food and how to store food. Food production and storage should be a focus not left in the hands of political leaders alone but a responsibility of all individuals, families and institutions including those that put themselves out to represent God. Developed nations should be able to lend their knowledge and skills to support food production, process, storage and services in developing nations. Families can lean how to milk cow supply milk for daily use etc. Departments for variety of food plants in a nations or country should be developed in universities. The real problem in developing nations is not natural food plants but lack of research, inventory of natural foods, process and storage facilities and infrastructures for variety of food production and sanitation requirements. This are things we should not expect God to do but we have to do ourselves.

The second natural need identified was land and shelter. In Genesis 2:15, the Lord took man and put him into the Garden of Eden to dress and to keep it.[96] Bruce Allsopp describes the garden as a small, ecologically balanced system in which man participated to his practical and aesthetic advantage.[97]

He defined the garden as "a plot of land devoted to the cultivation of flowers, fruit, and vegetables."[98] Gerhard von Rad adds that God planted a garden for man in Eden, which we must think of as a park of trees (Ezek. 13:8).[99]

J. W. Packer attempts to identify the place and the meaning of Eden. He believes Eden is the proper name of a land in the distant east. The word *Eden* appears in Hebrew as *Eden*, in Akksdian as *edinu*, and in Sumerian as *Eden*.[100]

Packer is convinced that the early Sumerians probably got the word *Eden* (a plain) from the fact that the original Eden was a flat, fertile tract.

In Hebrew, Eden became associated with the concept of "enjoyment" or "pleasure."[101]

Other biblical commentators identify Eden as a location in the east—a locality, not a symbol—although the same Hebrew word for Eden appropriately means "delight."[102] Eastward (Miqqedem) does not mean "from the East" but "in the East"; here, the Hebrew shows location.[103] Ackroyd et al. conclude that Eden was a place of particular beauty and reflects in so many details God's favor toward his chief creatures.[104] The Garden became a shelter or home for the first human family.

Shelter forms one of the basic needs of man's primeval history and constitutes man's earliest spatial environment. Today, shelter performs several functions, from protection against predators and privacy for biological activities to symbolic communication activities.

Land issues have become one of the leading causes of conflict between individuals and nations. History is full of examples of individuals or nations with unlawful occupational behaviors that they would hardly tolerate themselves on their own land. Land holds the key to site for settlement and resources. How we use land and who has access to land is a key issue in the world. Many of the land tax system are created in a way that those who cannot afford can always lose their dominion over the land to those who can afford. In some cities, it is hard to come by land for family expansion and housing development. The homeless issue has at its core land and shelter ownership issues. The poor lack the dominion to have access and control over land and shelter

Relationships

In Genesis 2:19–20, God brought every animal he made to Adam to see what Adam would call them. Adam gave names to all cattle, fowls of the air, and every beast of the field.

Merrill Unger made an interesting observation. God, who had pronounced each part of his creation work "good," soon realized it was not good for Adam to be alone without someone who looked just like him. God felt such a singleness was not necessary, and man, he thought, needed a companion or counterpart—someone to form a family with and to complement him physically, intellectually, and spiritually.[105]

God then decided to make him a companion. "I will make a help fit for him" (Hebrew., K^e neg dô, "as in his presence," meaning "one like himself" in the physical form).[106] True partnership is expounded by the description that is used (a helper for him; Gen. 2:18–20), which literally means "a help as opposite him"—that is, corresponding to him.

It seems the naming of animals, a scene that portrays man as monarch of all he surveys, poignantly reveals him as a social being made for fellowship, not power. He will not leave until he loves, giving himself away to another on his own level.[107]

Ackroyd, Leaney, and Packard suggest Genesis 2:21–25 opens with the recognition that man was incomplete and needed a partner or suitable helper.[108]

The creation of a woman was completed in a very extraordinary way. Unger points out that Eve was created not of the dust of the earth but from a rib of Adam.[109]

He explains the meaning of the word *rib* (*selāᶜ*), usually a "side," so the Septuagint renders the term by the pleura, denoting a piece of his side.[110] The word *made* literally means "built" or "constructed," suggesting extraordinary skill, care, and taste in the plan and proportion of the structure [111] Gen 2:22-23

The Hebrew word for "bone" (*esem*) signifies not only "body" or frame" but "essence". Adam and Eve were placed in the Garden of Eden, which became their home. Now that they were happily married, the union became an inseparable unit and fellowship of life with Adam, and the mode of her creation to lay an actual foundation for the moral ordinance of marriage. [112]

Adam and Eve shared a genetic makeup necessary in creating the environment of love and dedication for fulfilling themselves as they cleaved to each other, creating the environment vital for the spiritual and cultural growth of their progeny.[113]

Work and Rest

In Eden the couple had the responsibility of caring for the garden. It seems they were not only responsible for caring for and dressing the garden, but also for superintending the activities of the animals and birds. Work was tied to recreation than a profession or way of making a living.

Work was service-oriented and driven by a stream of love, attachment, and meaningful relationships. The benefit of work or labor cannot be over-emphasized today.

The Bible is clear on the relationship between labor and rest. Any attempt to emphasize one over the other may do a disservice to the effectiveness of the intent of the Bible. Man should work six days and rest on the seventh day. In our modern economy, the church that emphasized rest should also emphasize labor, job and job creation. Is not enough to develop a theology and a place for rest or worship and think your job is done. The challenge of job creation should occupy a central place in theology equally important as rest. The Bible has been clear that both has a place in creation man must labor and rest. When labor is applied to natural resources production takes place and life is change because individual can use labor to convert natural resources into goods and services to meet individual, family and national needs. The church stands to loose if it continues to fail in developing a sound theology of labor to educate and support individuals and families to fulfill the command to labor and rest.

In modern culture, private and public sectors depend on the use of human resources or labor energy for production of goods and services. However, we must be mindful of the cost of labor that drives the cost of goods and services up to a point where consumers cannot afford essentials goods and services because of the cost of labor.

The Third World and underdeveloped nations could do well if they were encouraged to use their raw materials at home for production of goods and services, which would generate job opportunities. Also, in cities across America, individuals should be educated and train to create jobs than to look for one. Present educational system is designed for individuals to look for job than to create one. Everybody can have a job if there is an education, training and structure in place to support individual job creation.

Because God requires man to labor and rest, the church has a leadership role to encourage and promote labor and rest. The bible is clear that six days we should labor and then rest on the seventh Exodus 20:8.

In Genesis 2:1–3, God completed his own work of creation in six days and then rested on the seventh day. The word *rest* clearly shows God working at some point and later ceasing after he was completed.

It seems man was created and wired for dominion, creativity, reproduction, companionship, bliss, labor, and rest.

Given the fact God was actively involved in the creation of man and his material environment and resources, the church can no longer live in isolation from its responsibility to lead humans to God and to provide insight into man as the created image of God with divine responsibility over the created world and resources through Jesus Christ.

The church also has a material responsibility toward the poor or those who have failed to develop adequate insight about themselves as the image of God with authority to exercise dominion over the natural resources entrusted to them for development. The church comes in as a "go-between" to teach moral economy, equal access, reasonable reward, and reasonable supply and demand and to ensure that those who reward themselves by making use of created existential resources will not deprive the rest of society access by asking for more rewards at the expense of the nation.

When man understands the reason and use of material resources than what it is presently use for man would have come to a better understanding that material resources were not meant for commercial interest, boosting individual or national ego or re-classifying the world into wealthy nations and none wealthy nations or industrial and none industrial nations.

The church must also play a role on the world stage to educate world leaders to understand the purpose of natural existential resources. As the population of the world continues to grow, the supply of resources will be limited. The industrial nations without adequate resources will converge in countries that have adequate resources but lack the required knowledge and skills to exercise dominion over their resources by putting in place the education, skills, research, investment and structure for dominion and socioeconomic development in the 21st century.

Chapter Ten

Genesian Foundation for Social Entrepreneurship

Just as natural resources are prospect for investment, education, research, job creation, business and socioeconomic development so is the crisis of Adam and Eve a good prospect for developing programs and services to respond to human crisis situations. We do not have to look too far for a good story line or look for example to explain why every human problem and crisis is an opportunity for service of some sought.

The problem of the fall of man, Adam and Eve in Genesis chapter three is an example of how we can respond in crisis situation and the services we bring along to help. As student of the Bible and therapist this same story has been relied on as the foundation for Christian theology, mission and ministries in the 20th century.

The good news is that as a bible student and therapist the same story of the fall also present from a crisis perspective and system theory a foundation for understanding the beginning of human problems and the basis for social entrepreneurship for 21st century. In fact we could go a step further to build up the case and the argument that other passages in the bible should be considered seriously the basis of social entrepreneurship. The Bible gives us a list of problems called the signs of the times including wars, hunger and pestilence in the last day.

The data result in chapter seven shows that there is consensus that the church has a role to play in helping individual find resources and deal with their crisis and needs. The church that preached problem should also announce or explains what people can do in case there is problem that no one can stop.

Human problems or crisis are an excellent opportunity to diversified services across race, tribe, tongues, people and nations. Individuals, families and nations must anticipate crisis and be prepared to put in place responses that will be needed to relieve distress. In many situations we are prepared for day-to-day need than we are prepared, ready and have in place crisis readiness training, programs and services.

Although God provided and met man's needs before and after human problems and needs continue to evolve. The first human family like many modern family met crisis and challenges. Crisis brings new problems, difficulties, challenges, needs, demands for immediate response program, social services and social entrepreneurship. The poor happen to be in the phase of crisis and challenges every day. The poor cannot afford resources or pay for basic resources or services to meet the challenges of everyday life, let alone crisis situation. If an individual, family or state can not meet the physical needs of people on a daily basis by providing the necessary resources how will the individual or state provide or respond in crisis. This is why assessing the level of human problems and unmet needs are very important for planning and pulling crisis resources together before crisis strikes.

The principle of crisis states that the severity of the crisis should be assessed from the client's subjective viewpoint and from the assessor's objective viewpoint and the Objective assessment of a crisis situation is based on an appraisal of the client's functioning in three areas: cognitive (thinking pattern), affective (feeling emotional tone), and psychomotor (behavior).[114]

Crisis could be described as a state of disintegration in which people face frustration of important life goals or profound disruption of their life cycles and methods of coping with stressors.[115]

Gilliland and James's definition also identified the four stages of crisis: (1) a critical situation occurs in which a determination is made as to whether a person's normal coping mechanisms will suffice; (2) increased tension and disorganization surrounding the event escalate beyond the person's coping ability; (3) a demand for additional resources to resolve the event is needed; and (4) a referral may be required to resolve major personality disorganization.[116]

Malcolm Payne points out that every person, group, and organization has crises and hazardous events (adolescence, marriage, or moving a household), unanticipated events (death, divorce, redundancy, and environmental disasters) [117] moral failure, poverty, or economic meltdown. Assessing Adam and Eve's fall or crisis will help us understand the problems and needs of Adam and Eve.

In the story of Adam and Eve, we have more than one problem that needed attention and interventions. To bring the problem to a more clear view I have to combine my theological knowledge and assessment skills using the system theory approach.

The system concept originated in the General System Theory of Bertalanffy. This system is a biological theory that proposes that all organisms are systems.[118]

The key idea of the system theory is that the effect on one part affects the whole. Beals states that life cannot be divided into neat, emotional aspects[119] but rather, there is integration in life that brings all the various parts together into a single entity, an entity that may reflect either wholeness or brokenness.[120]

The Adam and Eve Needs Assessment and Intervention Plan (AENAI) has been developed to create an understanding of the holistic problems of Adam and Eve and the problems that continue to plague modern families. The plan opens with a description of the life of the couple before they start having problem. The plan assessed how problems emerged, the losses they suffered and the intervention set in motion to relieve their problem. This assessment is consistent with the situation of all people in crisis whether spiritual, social, mental and physical crisis. The awareness of this insight should help us to understand that disobedience or breaking of the law or any relationship comes with other problem and does not matter if the relationship is with God or fellow human. Therefore, consideration should be giving to holistic assessment planning and intervention. Even if the church does not do anything but limit it self to Adam and Eve, it will still have to assess the full nature of the problem, life before the problem, the new needs arising out of the problem and the level of interventions, programs and services it will require to respond to Adam and Eve adequately.

AENAI Model of Human Crisis

Adam and Eve lived as a couple in a beautiful garden home east in Eden. Prior to their crisis, they had no children. Resource-wise, they were well-off and had an abundant supply of food, water, animals, gold, and precious minerals. The couple's relationship was good, including their health. The level of relationship with God, each other, and resources in their environment was good. The couple worked six days a week tending and keeping their environment. They functioned at an optimum level.

Old age was not a part of their development. However, this normal day-to-day life was cut short due to trouble with the law that warned against touching the forbidden tree and fruit. Let us look at the problem.

Presenting Problem

Adam and Eve were found guilty of violating a restriction that forbade them from eating of the Tree of the Knowledge of Good and Evil. Both were sentenced to die at some later date.

They lost everything they had and were asked to leave their home, never to return. They lost their garden home and direct contact with everything they had. Verbally, they blamed each other for their failure. Emotionally, they were afraid and hid themselves because they felt naked and ashamed. The experienced emotional sensed of guilt.

They had poor spiritual relationship with higher power, poor relationship with each other as each engaged in blaming and shifting blame not ready to take responsibility for their actions. The also experienced spiritual problem including the claim and belief they were influenced by another force similar to claims made by individual who claimed were influence d by a devil when they acted or commit a crime. Whether or not we believe the claim, they thought they had a real experience with a voice or being that controlled and command them to act contrary to the rule not to touch the forbidden tree. Therefore, going against the law got them into trouble with the law. Whether we believe this was real or disturbance in the senses the fact is that here we have the first recorded history or evidence that behavior can be influence by a force outside the human head or senses that could cause great problems in the victims.

Losses

Associated with their losses, they suffered emotional problems and exhibited maladaptive behavior identified and exhibited by running away, finding fault, blaming each other, and losing a caring attitude. Emotionally, they exhibited fear in God's presence; shame and regret; and, eventually, guilt, pain, nakedness, and anger.

Other losses identified include spiritual and moral decline, loss of control over mind, loss of labor, loss of stewardship or dominion, loss of land and resources, loss of a relationship with God, loss of life and health, loss of love, and loss of their garden home. The women would now give birth in pain, and the men would labor and sweat in the process to have access to food, which was free before the fall. The above problems demand immediate response.

Human problems did not end but were also felt elsewhere in creation. A study completed by Younker points out that Genesis 3 does not provide much information on the precise nature of the curses that took effect after the Fall.[120]

We know the serpent was cursed, the woman would experience pain in childbearing, and the ground would bring forth thorns and thistles.[121] In Younker's assessment, the implication of the curse brought out the fact that the woman and man are now at odds with each other (Gen. 3:17).

Also, the earth no longer willingly yields good trees for fruit (Gen. 1:12, 29). Indeed, it now also produces thorns and thistles, and Adam, Eve, and their descendants must struggle with it by the sweat of their brow (Gen. 3:8, 19).[122] In essence, man had become a slave to the earth he was created to dominate (Gen. 1:28). The animals God provided (1:24) would soon be in rebellion against man's dominion (6:1–13; 9:5–6). The earth from which God formed man would ultimately receive him in death (Gen. 3:19).[123]

Today, addressing similar problems will require specific knowledge, skills, and specialized programs and services. But let us look at their strengths.

Strengths

When Adam and Eve were asked to leave, they had access to land outside of Eden. They had water and other material resources. They were physically capable and energetic. They were blessed with light and the assurances of a Savior or Gospel.

God acted like a therapist and resources person. He address every aspect of the impact of their behavior, emotional problems, worries, clothing needs, relationship, change in work routine, child birth issues, relationship with spiritual forces and hope of a plan, a savior, that will deliver them and succeeding generation from the impact of their disobedience or violation. They were clothed and remained in the image and likeness of God. Adam and Eve loved each other, were capable of childbearing. They had knowledge of good and evil, ability to have dominion, to enjoy and work with resources in their environment and surroundings.

Therefore, solution to Adam and Eve problems required a comprehensive response and resources. We now see from the assessment that the fall was not only a spiritual issue or problem but it affected all dimensions of Adam and Eve life, function and relationship with God, each other and the material world.

Therefore, the scope of Christian theology, mission and ministry will have to be broadened to reflect the scale of the problem and the levels of interventions required to effect change and improve the function of man. The benefit of the AENAI plan could not be overemphasized in the process of helping us understand the holistic nature of Adam and Eve problem and succeeding generation.

The need for re-interpreting Christian theology to reflect real life problems and realities will continue to hunt Christian mission and ministry from generation to generation until a more holistic response is developed.

Biblical Crisis Programs and Services

Human needs have been central to the biblical worldview since creation. God was equally responsive to the crisis needs of Adam and Eve by providing message of hope (Gen. 3:15) and animal skin clothing to replace the leaf coverings the wore (Gen. 3:20). The concept of "the poor" occupies a central place.

In the Old Testament, the word *ani*, meaning "poor, weak; afflicted; humble,"[124] takes on different meanings, depending on the context in which it is used. The noun *ani* can be used synonymous with *ebyon* (needs) and *dal* (poor).[125]

The word *poor* describe a physical condition and sometimes mean "poor in spirit." In the context of the latter, the word describes those who, because of their condition in this world, are dependent on and have turned to God.[126]

A contrast exists between the latter and the former usage of the expression "poor man." The adjective may refer to one that has become exhausted, wasted, and weak in substance or natural strength, as opposed to the former usage of the word in Leviticus 19:15.[127] In that context, the word *poor* in the former usage implies one that is miserable, helpless, and despised.

The idea is that the Bible takes into account man's material conditions and spiritual needs. The Bible has never attempted to play one against the other or make the latter more important than the former. The Bible has always made man's holistic condition central to biblical mission and ministry.

In Genesis 45:11 the word *poverty* relates to want. In this context, Joseph promised to minister, sustain, and provide for his family. The purpose was to prevent a household or family from coming to poverty and want.

In the book of Job (24:1–21; 31:16–23), the poor are described as those kicked aside, those who spend all their time getting enough to keep body and soul together, going in search of food for their children, going about naked, and being forced to carry food while they themselves are starving and not getting help.

Because man's material needs were central to God's creation, specific instructions are found in the Old Testament about responding to human needs. These responses are in the form of intervention. In Deuteronomy 15:8–10, the poor are to be released from their debts, and resources are to be shared freely with the poor. Since man cannot have access to material resources without money, the demand for money will continue to rise (including the demand for work to make a living), and debt will continue to multiply as many cannot earn enough or are forced to earn less and stay in debt to have access to basic life resources. Those who benefit are those who continue to dominate the use of natural resources in production of goods and services.

Therefore, in the political and religious example of governance and policy making, the nation of Israel was required to support the Levites, foreigners, orphans, and widows in towns and cities from the tithe given to the Levites (Deut. 14:28–29). Intervention is critical to helping those in need. This rule shows the Bible's concern and response to man's spiritual relationship as well as his material needs.

In creation, God was actively involved in providing basic human needs. After the Fall, he responded to Adam and Eve's clothing needs and announced the gospel (Gen. 3:15, 20). One wonders whether the Savior spoken of in Genesis 3:15 pays particular attention to human needs.

It comes as no surprise that Jesus paid particular attention to human needs at two levels: spiritual and material. In Luke 4:16, Christ's mission is described in more general and broader terms.

The narrative in Mark gives a more concise and dramatic picture of Christ's physical involvement with people. He was engaged not only in preaching, but also in a feeding and healing ministry (the feeding of the five thousand [Mark 6:33–44], feeding of the four thousand [Mk 8:11–21], healing of the blind man [Mk 8:11–21]). This is consistent with what life would have looked like if man had kept God's law.

The narrative in Luke describes a number of stories that underscore Christ's response to individual problems. Christ focused on man's material, physical, and spiritual needs. The texts best illustrating this principle include the feeding of the five thousand (Lk 9:10–17), ministries to the sick, the healing of Peter's mother-in-law (4:38–39), the healing in the evening (Lk 4:40–41), the healing of the Garrison demoniac, the woman with the hemorrhage, and Jairus's daughter.

Christ also addressed other issues including anxiety (Lk 12:22–34) and fear (Lk 12:1–12). In John's gospel, we find the feeding of the crowd (Jn 6:1–14), the marriage and family at Cana (Jn 2:1–12), and more healing ministries.

Acts provides valuable information about human needs, the level of attention paid to human needs, and services in the first Christian church, which is consistent with Jesus mission and ministry practice.

The book of Acts gives us an insight into the background of the birth of the early church in Jerusalem. Although preaching and the expansion of the church remained a key focus, the church was also involved in community social ministry. Money owned by the church was distributed according to the needs of the people (Acts 4:35).

However, as the church progressed, some felt it was no longer the duty of the church to respond to physical and material needs. This did not play well among the Christian leaders.

The book of James helps us to understand the tension between a Christianity that emphasizes preaching as its primary mission and a Christianity that emphasizes other aspects of man's life. James seems to combat the artificial distinction drawn between physical and spiritual needs and emphasizes practical holiness (2:14–17).

First Christian Crisis Response Team

What kind of programs and services did the early Christians provide? Early Christians were very practical about the centrality of care in the mission and ministry of the church.

They refused to believe or view themselves as a "communion of souls" whose only concern was each other's spiritual welfare. The bodily and material needs of members were just as much a corporate responsibility. The duty was not delegated to the state or local agencies.

Systems for providing human needs and emotional support were well in place. For those living within Christian households, their needs were met within a family context.[128]

In the New Testament, households were given the obligation to provide for their immediate dependents, including slaves, as well as relatives, especially the widows who had been deprived of their means of support.[129]

Visiting

Although the problems could not always be removed, a number of different ways were available through which help might come. Visiting orphans and widows in their affliction and those who were imprisoned and ill-treated was one way.

Prayer

Prayer for the sick, accompanied by some physical gestures such as anointing with oil, raising by touch, or laying on of hands were others (John 5:14–16; cf. Acts 2:3–8; 9:17; 14:1).

Healing

Exercise of various gifts of healing also took place. Occasional miraculous works were also noted when members of the community were gifted in these ministries (1 Cor. 12:9–10, 28; Gal. 3–5).

The church also provides material support. For example, if there is a real widow, one left all alone with no one to provide for her, the church is to step in and look after her needs (1 Tim. 5:16).

We must also remember that it was not only the lack of money, food, clothing, and other such necessities that concerned the early Christian church. Loneliness, physical disability, and illness of members were also communal concerns.

Work or employment was another form of providing for one's need. Ministers encouraged those who previously relied on the customary handouts of wealthier patrons for their livelihood to overcome the pervasive Greek tendency to despise the manual work and to, instead, find employment to support their family. Welfare support should not undermine individual or a family dominion. Individual must be offered the opportunity to have independence economically. It is clear due to scarcity of jobs not everyone can be employed in their job of interest. However, we should be thinking of giving opportunities to others to use their skills when the regular work force is on vacation or during the summer.

Paul admonished his readers to "work with your own hands" (1 Thess. 4:11). He wanted workers to earn the respect of outsiders and to be dependent on nobody (2 Thess. 3:10–12).

So, in a number of ways, the early churches possessed the means for looking after most of the physical and material needs of their members, as well as friends and strangers who visited them.

The church also paid attention to the needs of associated communities else where.[130]

It could be said that in the Jerusalem church, not a needy person was among them (Acts 4:34).

Chapter Eleven

Theological Foundation for Faith-based Socioeconomic Development

Bosch Mission Insight

Bosch states that since the nineteen fifties, there has been a remarkable escalation in the use of the word *mission* among Christians.[131]

The word *mission* includes several activities: (a) the sending of missionaries, (b) activities undertaken by such missionaries, (c) geographical areas, (d) the agency which sends the missionaries, (e) the non-Christian world or "mission field," (f) the center from which the missionaries operated on the "mission field," (g) a local congregation, and (h) a series of special services intended to enhance or spread the Christian faith.[132]

In the sixteenth century, the term *mission* was used to describe the doctrine of the Trinity. Bosch states that this traditional interpretation of mission, with emphasis on communication about the seed of the woman, Jesus Christ, has gradually been modified in the course of the twentieth century.

The reason for this modification was due to the fact that the church in general, and Christian mission in particular, are today confronted with issues they have never even dreamed of, or ignored, which are crying out for responses that are both relevant to the times and in harmony with the essence of the Christian faith.[133]

The demand for material mandate or cultural mandate has increased alongside the spiritual mandate. Several factors account for this as follows: People in all parts of the world are striving for freedom and dominion. There are unjust structures of oppression and exploitation of resources that impede progress to dominion and freedom. More than ever before, we know that material resources are finite in supply. We know that people and their environments are mutually interdependent.

Therefore, Bosch states that it is impossible to think of the church without thinking, in the same breath, of the world to which it is sent.[134] Breakthrough occurred when the Vatican II Pastoral Constitution of the

Church recognized an intimate link that goes far beyond evangelism and church planting. Therefore, the church's attitude is the joy and hope, grief and anguish of the people of our times, especially of those who are poor or afflicted in any way.

How does the material and spiritual mandate fit within the mission and faith-based social services of the church? First, the church can no longer be viewed as the ground of mission, let alone be considered the goal of mission. The church should represent the glory of God intended at creation.

Second, the church is not the kingdom of God. The church on earth is the seed of God's intended reign in Eden and the beginning of that kingdom. Third, the church's missionary involvement suggests more than calling individuals into the church as a waiting room for the hereafter. Those to be evangelized are, with other human beings, subject to social, economical, and political conditions in the world.[135] Bosch also emphasized the spiritual role of the church. He states the church is to be viewed pneumatologically as a dwelling place of God in the spirit.

Recovery Insight

Each mandate, spiritual or material, requires a holistic recovery approach for effective response. The complexity of human problems will require complex approaches, services and programs to respond. This is why the past mistakes of spiritualizing all aspect of human life, problems and needs from Adam and Eve to succeeding generation is not consistent with biblical salvation. God created a real world, real people, real place and resources for human dominion. The biblical concept of salvation and recovery is consistent with reality. When we think of the many Individuals and families facing spiritual and socioeconomic problems on day-to-day experience what is salvation like? Is salvation a spiritual matter or a holistic dimensional matter that affect spiritual, physical, mental and social dimension of man and require holistic approach?

Salvation means preservation from threat, impending deserved danger, and suffering. Salvation is used in the New Testament as material and temporal deliverance from danger and apprehension.[136] The word reflects different situations or events of daily life from which people are saved: national events (Luke 1:9, 71); personal deliverance, as from the sea (Acts 27:34); and safety, health, and care in prison (Phil 1:19) and during flood (Heb 11:17).

Above all, it includes spiritual and eternal deliverance granted immediately by God to those who accept his conditions of repentance and faith in the Lord Jesus.

Salvation is also used to describe any kind of human situation or problem in which a person is delivered from spiritual, social, physical, or mental stress as well as danger, whether real or potential.[137]

The word *sozo*, "to save," is sometimes used to mean "healing" or "restoration to health"—the latter in John 11:12, "he will recover," "saved," or "shall do well." Sozo is also used to express a return to soberness, as from a state of delirium or drunkenness.[138]

Therefore, the recovery model of salvation does not presume a single model or intervention to solve human problems. Salvation is a multidimensional, systematic approach to human problems and challenges in recovery.

The recovery model includes a holistic view of individuals and a self-managed approach to interventions necessary to return fallen man to some minimal stability. In addition, the recovery model of salvation emphasizes a need for holistic understanding of human problems and the rights of individuals to experience salvation in all dimensions of their lives.

John Bennett writes that the word *salvation* denotes a condition of a person's life in all his relationships that are directly experienced in this world.[139] Table 15 below gives us a list of human problems the researcher compiled from the Fall of Adam and Eve giving rise to the argument that salvation can not be limited to spiritual intervention alone but a holistic approach. Similar argument hold true in all social support and healing programs that provides human services to individuals and families. Every individual should have a recovery plan in place.

Table 15

The AENAMS Assessment Recovery Plan

Name (City area or Target Population):

Problems Index	Needs	L/S	Goals	Program	Target Date	Date Resolved
Adam & Eve Eviction Gen 3:23,24	Place of habitation/Dwelling	S	Promote affordable housing development	Housing program		
Naked Gen 3:10	Clothing	S	Reduce appearance of naked-ness, nudity Gen 3:21,28	Clothing program		
Hard Work Gen 3:17-18	Mechanical eq2uipment & work	L	Reduce hard labor & promote work skills & tools Gen 3:23	Job program		
Painful childbirth Gen 3:16	Prenatal & delivery care	L	Reduce painful child delivery & risk	Fruitful care ma-ternity program		
Exhibit paranoia Gen 3:8	Spiritual development & therapy Promote hope	L	Increase spiritual relationship with God on personal basis	Psych program Church program		
Theft Gen 2:17; 3:6	Moral development & therapy	L	Encourage moral development with emphasis on ten com-mandments & society laws	Law & Order pro-gram		
Physical deterioration & death Gen 3:19; 5:5	Medical care & funeral arrange-ments & bereavement therapy	L	Promote & maintain good health, comfort the bereaved & support the widow	Bereavement pro-gram		
Food plant				Food program		

Church Insight

A key contribution of this report is the compilation of theological responses by church leaders and their contributions to community and social ministry theology for faith-based programs and services.

For more than one hundred years, the Church has sponsored social welfare ministry, disaster relief, and public health services in North America and around the world. [140]

What theological support informed the church's response? Church member viewed the church as a concerned body created for service. Christ's followers are called to serve the Lord in praise, serve one another in love, and serve the world in humility.[141]

The inspirational support for the church Community Social Ministry came out of the early writings on welfare ministry by one of the church leading member, White. White seemed to hold a balanced understanding of man's natural needs, human nature, and social order or problems.

She would agree with many sociologists that man is by nature a social being.[142] White was also aware of the impact of the laws on human social needs and development—these laws she identified as *natural laws.*

"All nature is in the fullest sense under the control of physical law."[143] The material world is under the control of the laws that govern nature. She called these laws the laws of life and moral laws.

The laws of life: The laws of life are the laws of physiology, nutrition, and hygiene, as well as those principles that promote and preserve good physical well-being.

White believed that it is the duty of every person, for his or her own sake and for the sake of humanity, to inform oneself in regard to the laws of life and to conscientiously obey them.[144] You cannot be reminded too often that health does not depend on chance.[145]

Moral laws: Let it be made plain that the way of God's commandment is the way of life. Every "thou shall not," whether in physical or moral law, implies a promise. If we obey, blessings will attend our steps.[146]

White also called upon the Church to be sensitive to distress and problems encountered by individuals or families. She states that "poverty and distress in families will come to our knowledge, and afflicted and suffering ones will have to be relieved."[147]

She also stated that none should receive the idea that the poor and unlearned are to be neglected. She described social conditions in large cities: "In these cities, there are multitudes of human beings who do not receive as much care and consideration. There are thousands of children, ragged and half starved, with vice and depravity written on their faces."[148]

Also, White was concerned about families who were herded together in miserable tenements, many of them in cellars reeking with dampness and filth, impure words, fumes of liquor and tobacco, and moral degradation. All of these things meet the eyes and perverts the senses. She commented that from these abodes of wretchedness, piteous cries for food and clothes are sent out by many who know nothing about prayer.

White adds further insights into Jesus line of work. She states, "Our Savior went from house to house healing the sick, feeding the hungry, Matt. 19:3, comforting the mourners, soothing the afflicted, speaking peace to the disconsolate."[149]

It seems that she had holistic views of sin and its impact. She stated that in the mission and ministry of the church, the work in large cities had not been as well organized as other churches have done, and the methods of labor hadn't been efficient enough to reflect the holistic impact of sin and its problems.

This may be because so many church ministers have been those who love to preach, so a large share of ministry has been put forth in preaching.[150] White stressed that no man, whether a teacher, a physician, or a minister, can ever hope to be completely whole. She felt that God ordained many skills needed in God's service in order that the talents of many minds could be blended.[151]

She further underscored biblical holism and stressed that total evangelism, mission, and ministry are required in the great cities in North America and that different human service agencies are to be set to work.[152] Therefore, every facility for the advancement of the work of ministry should be put into use.[153] The practical question is what role should this information play in family, theology, ministry, education, career choices, business training and political leadership? Should it influence our ideas and practice or help guide practice and policy making for socioeconomic development, entrepreneurship, social services and educational training, research and investment? Also, what are the best ways of articulating the information in real life experience and community and social development? Who is best at handling it and implementing it for the good of all the government, private individuals, religious institutions or business leaders or educational authorities? One thing is clear socioeconomic changes and entrepreneurship can not be brought about by rioting, guns, killings, resistance and avoidance. It can only occur in people that have developed awareness of their true identity and the role and responsibilities link to their identity awareness. This is consistent with the teachings in Genesis 1and 2, the fact God link human role and responsibilities to subdue the earth and it resources and dominion to human identity, the image and likeness of God, a concept developed by Moses when he was in Egypt, Africa. The fact today is that the average person is less prepared to deal and respond with knowledge and skills to problems and challenges in his environment than Adam and Eve where equipped with knowledge and skills to subdue the earth and have dominion. May be the role of specialization has contributed to that or the very issue we have discussed through out this book the position of some religion and leaders to keep seeking God and doing what God expects and reward of salvation from the expectation to subdue the earth and it resources and maintain dominion from religion. The call to unite God, man, subdue and maintain dominion in the world under God can not be less of a far cry and need today than any time in history. We have seen and experience the result and impact when we forced separation in things that were not separated causing unnecessary isolation and lack of better equipped individuals with shared dimensions.

The challenge for all systems and institution religious, political, educational, business including Wall street and Main street is how to bring all of these institutions combined with human resources into human development an approach lacking in the Twentieth-century.

Thanks to the fact that some countries are beginning to take a lead in human socioeconomic development and entrepreneurship. It is my hope that as the book and information continues to spread individuals will pass it on and used it to improve human condition globally.

Chapter Twelve

Summary and Conclusion

In a 1988 article, Sahlin stated that the church community social ministry in centers in the North American Division had declined, as evidenced by job cuts in community ministry.[154] Also, Gavin cited a considerable decline in commitment to community social ministry. [155]

The research proposal was developed to investigate and test the generalization by Sahlin and Gavin in a church field site or conference in Michigan. A research questionnaire was developed and sent to the church conference office with return envelop. The church distributed the questionnaire to church leaders and individuals directly involved with community social ministry programs and services.

In response to issues in the generalization (a decline in the number of centers), a total of 53 percent of respondents strongly agreed or agreed their churches have community centers with active programs and services in these centers.

On the issue of cuts in community ministry leadership, 43 percent of respondents strongly agreed, and 36.7 percent agreed that their churches have community social ministry leaders. This is a total of 79.9 percent.

46 percent of respondents strongly disagreed, and another 33.3 percent disagreed with the notion that salvation is all about spirituality. This is a total of 79.3 in favor of holistic salvation including the physical, mental, spiritual and social dimension of man.

20 percent of respondents strongly rejected the notion that by being involved in community social ministry, one may deviate from the gospel ministry; an additional 50 percent also disagreed. This is a total 70 percent of respondent agreed pastors should get involved in social ministry as part of their calling.

50 percent of respondents were strongly of the opinion that community social ministry is an effective means of witnessing in the community, and another 43.3 percent also shared similar views—a total of 93 percent of respondents are in favor using community ministry as a witnessing opportunity.

20 percent of respondents have a good understanding that the church has a mandate and a ministry to care for individuals and family in need, a view shared by another 43 percent. This is a total 63 percent of the total respondents.

A total of 83.3 percent of respondents agreed, to various degrees, that they also have a spiritual mandate to enable and empower people to establish a relationship with God.

The data analysis shows the individuals who volunteered to participate in the study are in favor of community social development and ministry. Also, they have a balance theological view of holistic gospel as the future or 21st direction of ministry.

However, a significant revelation is that the responses indicate that the majority of respondents do not attend annual training in community ministry. There were 46 percent of respondents who indicated that they do not attend annual training; only 20 percent do.

What is it that we do not know that will explain the reason for lack of training or support training? The researcher used a new approach borrowed from system theory to assess the book of Genesis chapter 1-3 used for historical justification for spiritual ministry to develop support socioeconomic development and social entrepreneurship. The application of system theory and assessment principles and skills demonstrated that a lot of issues were overlooked by church leaders when interpreting the same chapter.

Concluding Thesis

The study shows that the generalization of Sahlin and Gavin does not apply within the group studied. The data show that respondents are involved and support community social ministry by various programs and services. The data also shows that respondents are aware of the two mandates of mission, the material or cultural mandate and the spiritual or evangelistic mandate.

The data shows that the beliefs and practices of the respondents are consistent with biblical principles. The principle is always clear that a holistic approach to mission is the best Christian mandate.

However, a significant fact in the study is the need for training and preparing individuals and families holistically to engage and have dominion over the material resources in their environments and develop a relationship with God, the giver of these resources.

The church must learn from how God relates to mankind by providing natural resources, moral development or obedience, rest and worship. The church has to train and educate it work force about the values of man as the image and likeness of God created to exercise dominion. The state must also train it workers delivering social services or any other services to craft policies, programs and services that will have the goal of helping man experience what it means to live like the image of God and to have dominion. The level of training will off-set the problems we have in a system historically designed to degrade one another by stereotypes, poor policies, poor program and services that frustrate human holistic development and dominion.

It is hope by reading this book we can make changes to theological, socioeconomic training, programs, services and policies to assist all individuals to start at very early age to understand their identity and dominion responsibility. This will eradicate the wide spread human problems of de-humanizing one another in an attempt to dominate. It will also eradicate the limitation religion has placed on God as the spiritual leaders than appreciating the universal role of God in providing all human and material resources. The principle is clear Faith-based socioeconomic and social entrepreneurship will engage the world meaningfully consistent with the biblical creation declaration that God in the beginning created man in his image and likeness though fractured by trans-generational disobedience to have dominion restored through Jesus Christ transforming inwardly fallen man to a more obedient individual with dominion over the material world and it resources.

The Twenty-first century demands a new theoretical orientation, approach and emphais on human developmet. The centuries before was marked with less emphasis on human developmet, human identity and responsibilities to subdue the earth and it resources and have shared and collective deomion to rule, govern and domimate the earth. Instead, we witnessed less social development, identity development and opportunites for all. The religious institutions were interested in saving soals and preparing individuals for the orther world than be taught about their identity as the image and likeness of God with collective responsibilities to subdue the earth, it resources for education, career development, research, invention, job creation and wealth sharing. Business world was constructed on wealth for few, sterotypes between who is the richest and the poorest than scioeconomic development and social entreprenuurship. People were more or less going to school to find job than to create jobs giving the vast abundance of natural resources for innovation and business opportunities. Political leadership was more centered on power dispaly than on nation and human development and entrepreneurship. But the Twnety-firts centity has presented it self with unique opportunity forcing religious, poltical, educational and businness institutions to re-think their reason for existance as people are asking and demanding answers who am I, what should I be doing and what should we be doing togeather, is God concern about my well being, prosperity and development or not? What about religious and political leaders. Answers to these questions will demand different way of thinking and doing business as relgious, political, educational and business leaders and families than waht we thought we exisit for and should be about past centuries. The question is who is ready to take the challenage, re-think, start and take the lead in human development, socioeconomc development and entrepreneurship and how? The principle is clear human responsibilities to subdue the earth, it resources and have dominion is link to human identity. Therefore, without clear insight into ones true identity economic and social development can not occure.

Endnotes

Chapter 1

[1] John Gavin, "Adventist Service," term paper, 27 April 1992, 10.

[2] Monte Sahlin, "Adventist Community Services," *Adventist Review*, 5 May 1988, 21.

[3] Ibid.

[4] "Hospital Asked to Provide Constant Care for Donor," Benton Harbor (Michigan), *The Herald Palladium,* October 1998, 7a

[5] General Conference of Seventh-day Adventist, Washington DC.), *Bulletin of Symposium on Mission and Social Action,* October 10–11, 1997 (Silver Springs, MD)

[6] Robert, C, Siegal, H and Falck, R, *Qualitative Research Methods in Drugs and AIDS Prevention Research: An Overview* Bethesda, Maryland. US Department of Health and Human Services and National Institute on Drug Abuse. Retrieved from PsycEXTRA database, 1995

[7] C. E. Moustakes, Phenomenological Research Methods (Thousand Oaks, CA: Sage Publication, 1994), p

Chapter 3

[8] Security: Social Insurance, http://www.cas.michco.edu/security/tourb.htm1996

[9] Wilter J. Cohen, "Social Welfare Programs," *The Encyclopedia Americana,* (1998), vol. 25, 139.

[10] Ibid

[11] Ibid

[12] "Hospital Asked to Provide Constant Care for Donor," Benton Harbor (Michigan), *The Herald Palladium,* October 1998, 7a.

[13] Ibid

[14] National Internet Clearing House (NICH), *Welfare Reform at the Federal, State, and Local Levels,* Wayne County, MI. http://www.com/hp/nwr/mi26163.html, 1997.

[15] Ibid

[16]   Ibid

Chapter 4
[17]   H.R. Niebuhr and Yeager, "The Social Gospel and the Mind of Jesus".
       Journal of Religious Ethics. 16, no. 1 1998, 109-127
[18]   Walter Rauschenbusch, A Theology for Social Gospel (New York:
       Abingdon Press, 1917).
[19]   Ibid
[20]   Elmore O. Vernon, Layman's Library of Christian Doctrine (Nashville:
       Broadman Press, 1986).
[21]   Ibid
[22]   Ibid
[23]   Ibid
[24]   Ibid
[25]   Frances Nigel Lee, The Origin and Destiny of Man (NewJersy:
       Presbyterian and Reformed Press, 1977).
[26]   Elmore
[27]   Ibid
[28]   Ibid
[29]   Sinclair B. Ferguson and David F. Wright, New Dictionary of Theology
       (Avon, Great Britain: The Bath Press, 1994).
[30]   Ibid
[31]   John R. Sachs, The Christian Vision of Humanity (Minneapolis: The
       Liturgical Press, 1991).

Chapter 5
[32]   David O. Moberg, *The Great Reversal* (Philadelphia: J.B. Lippincott
       Company, 1977), 13.
[33]   Ibid.
[34]   Ibid.
[35]   Ronald J. Snider, *One-sided Christianity*, (Grand Rapids: Zondervan
       Publishing House, 1993),167.
[36]   Ibid.
[37]   Bruce Nicholls, *In Word and Deed: Evangelism and Social Responsibility*
       (Exeter: The Paternoster Press, 1985), 7.

38 Bruce Bradshaw, *Bridging the Gap* (Monrovia, CA: MARC, 1992), 6, 7.
39 Ibid.

Chapter 6

40 Louis Badillo, "A Survey of the Social Gospel and Seventh-day Adventist in the 1890s and Early 1900s," *Review and Herald,* 24 May 1973, 6.
41 L. A. Smith, "The Hopelessness of the Effort to Reform Politics." *Review and Herald,* 6 April 1905, 5.
42 Ibid.
43 Ibid.
44 Jonathan Butler, "City of Big Shoulders," *Insight,* 11 August 1970, 14.
45 Mitchell A. Tyner, "The Church and Society," *Adventist Review, 4 January 1990, 14–15.*
46 Robert C. Linthicum, Empowering the Poor *(Monrovia, CA: Ventura Publisher, 1991), 21–23.*
47 Ibid.
48 Ibid
49 Ibid.
50 General Conference of Seventh-day Adventist, General Conference Bulletin, 2, 8, (29 October 1882): 2.
51 Ibid.
52 Jonathan Butler, Insight, "City of Big Shoulders," *Adventist Review,* August 1970, 3.
53 Karen Stockton Chilson and Mike Preas, "Involvement in Compassion Ministries," unpublished paper (College Place, WA: Walla Walla College, 1980), 3.
54 William G. Johnson, "Christians in A Needy World,"*Adventist Review,* May 1988, 3.
55 Ibid.
56 Ibid.
57 Ibid.
58 Charles Bradford, "Hunger and the Caring Church,"*Adventist Review,* May 1988, 17.

[59] Ibid.

[60] Myron Widmer, "What the Adventist Church Is Doing About Poverty," *Adventist Review,* May 1988, 19.

[61] Ibid.

[62] Ibid.

[63] Nelson C. Wilson, "Global Strategy and the Poor," *Adventist Review,* May 1988, 5.

[64] Calvin B. Rock, "Did Ellen White Downplay Social Work?" *Adventist Review,* May 1988, 6.

[65] Ibid

[66] Ivan Leigh Warden, "Cities," *Adventist Review,* 5 May 1998, 13.

Chapter 8

[67] A.P. Conrad, "Social Ministry in the Early Church: An Integrated Component of the Christian Community," *Social Thought 5,* no. 23 (Spring 1980), 41.

[68] Delos Miles, *Evangelism and Social Involvement* (Nashville: Broadman Press, 1986), 16.

[69] Diana S. Richmond Garland, "The Church as a Context for Social Work Practice," *RE,* 85 (1988), 255.

[70] Ibid.

[71] Donald K. Gorrell, *The Age of Social Responsibility: The Social Gospel in the Progressive Era 1900–1920* (Macon, GA: Mercer University Press, 1988), 58.

[72] John C. Bennett, *Social Salvation* (New York: Charles Scribner's Sons, 1948), xi.

[73] William Nicholls, *Confronting Images of Man* (New York: Seabury Press, 1966), 5.

[74] Sun Herald Online (Internet) Smith "Church Finds a Vision in Traditional Role of Social Services," http://www.sunherald.com/living/docs/vision0215.htm by Marquita Smith, 193.

[75] Ibid.

[76] Ibid.

[77] Caleb Rosado, "The Name of Society and the Challenge to Mission," *International Review of Mission 77* (January 1988), p.35.

[79] Edgar J. Ellison, *Christian Relief and Demographics* (Waco, TX: Word Publishing, 1989), 45.

80 Ibid.
81 Gorrell, 58.
82 John C. Bennett, Ibid.

Chapter 9

83 *The New International Dictionary of the Bible* (1987), s.v., "Genesis."
84 Ibid.
85 *Seventh-day Adventist Bible Dictionary* (1960), s.v., "Genesis."
86 Ibid.
87 Jean M. Hisberger, *The Catholic Bible,* (New York: Oxford University Press, 1995), 3.
88 John Leigh, *Land Life* (Los Angeles, CA: University of California Press, 1963), 155.
89 George R. Berry, *The Interlinear Literal Translation of the Hebrew Old Testament* (PA: Handy Book Corporation, 1897), 4.
90 Terry A. Armstrong, *Hebrew English Lexicon of the Old Testament* (Grand Rapids, MI: Zondervan, 1989), 3.
91 Nelson, 41.
92 Ekhard E. Ziegler and L. J. Filer, Jr., *Present Knowledge in Nutrition* (Washington, DC.: International Life Science Institute Press, 1996), 1.
93 Ibid.
94 Ibid.
95 Marion C. Linder, *Nutritional Biochemistry and Metabolism* (New York: n.p., 1985), 201.
96 Ibid., 203.
97 Ibid.
98 Berry, George R., *The Interlinear Literal Translation of the Hebrew Old Testament,* Grand Rapids, MI: Zondervan, 1943.
99 Bruce Allsopp, *The Garden Ecology* (New York: Morrow, 1972), 42.
100 Allsopp, Ibid.
102 Gerhard van Rad, *Genesis* (Philadelphia: The Sem Press, 1972), 84.
103 P.R. Ackroyd, A.R.C. Leaney and J. W. Packer, *The Cambridge Bible Commentary* (Cambridge: Great Britain, 1973), 36.
104 Ibid.
105 Deker Kidner, *Genesis* (Chicago: Intervarsity Press, 1967), 66.
106 Ackroyd, Leaney, and Packer, 12.

[107] Ackroyd, Leaney, and Packer, Ibid.

[108] Merrill F. Unger, *Unger Commentary on the Old Testament,* vol. 1(New York: Doubleday & Company, 1975), 13.

[109] Ibid.

[110] C. F. Keil and D.F. Delitzsch, *Bible Commentary on the Old Testament* (Grand Rapids, MI: Eerdmans, 1952), 89.

[111] Ackroyd, Leaney, and Packer, 36.

[112] Keil and Delitzsch, 89.

[113] Unger, 14.

Chapter 10

[114] Ibid.

[115] Keil and Delitzsch, 89.

[116] David Liebman, *The Eternal Torah* (NJ: Pines Press, 1979), 12.

[117] Donoso Escobar and Gary Hutchinson, "The 1996 Social Welfare Reform: What Does It Mean for Family Ministries?" *Journal of Family Ministry 11,* no. 2 (Spring 1997): 4.

[118] *Webster's Dictionary* (1997), s.v., "Assessment."

[119] Burl E. Gilliland and Richard K. James, *Handbook of Cognitive Behavioral Therapist* (CA: Brook and Cole Publishing, 1997), 34.

[120] Ibid.

[121] Ibid., 3.

[122] Gilliland and James, 3.

[122] Malcolm Payne, *Modern Social Work Theory* (Chicago: Lyceum Books, 1997), 99.

[123] Ibid., 137.

[124] Arthur Beals, *Beyond Hunger: A Biblical Mandate for Societal Responsibility* (Portland, OR: Multnomah Press, 1985), 84.

[124] Ibid.

[125] The General Conference of Seventh-day Adventist, *Adult Sabbath School Bible Study Guide,* Sabbath School, Personal Ministries Department, God's Creation (Nampa, ID: Pacific Press, 1999), 78.

[126] The General Conference of Seventh-day Adventist, Ibid.

[127] Ibid.

[128] Ibid.

Chapter 11

129 Bosch, David J., *Transforming Mission* (Maryknoll, New York: Orbis Books, 1991), 1.

130 Ibid.

131 Ibid.

132 Ibid.

133 Ibid.

134 Ibid., 378.

135 W. E. Vines, *Dictionary of Bible Words* (Nashville, TN: Thomas Nelson, 1999), 325.

136 Sinclair B Ferguson, et.al., "Salvation," *New Dictionary of Theology* (Leicester, England: Intervarsity Press, 1988), 610.

137 Vines, 304.

138 W. E. Vine, Merrill F. Unger, and William White, Jr., *Vines Expository Dictionary of Biblical Words* (Nashville, TN: Thomas Nelson, 1985), 180.

139 Sinclair B. Ferguson and David F. Wright, *New Dictionary of Theology* (Avon, England: Bath Press, 1988), 523.

140 W. E. Vine, Merrill F. Unger, and William White, Jr., *Vine's Expository Dictionary of Biblical Words* (Nashville, TN: Thomas Nelson, 1985), 180.

141 Ibid.

142 Ferguson, and Wright, Ibid., 523.

143 William Wilson, *Old Testament Word Studies* (Peabody, MA: Hendrickson Publisher), p. 317.

144 Robert Bank, "The Early Church as a Caring Community," *Evangelical Review of Theology*, no. 1 (April 1983), 310.

145 Ibid.

146 *Bible Principle,* 1990, North American Division of Seventh-day Adventist, Silver Springs, MD.

147 *Bible Principle, Ibid.*

148 Ibid.

148 Ellen G. White, *Patriarchs and Prophets* (Mountain View, CA: Review and Herald, 1958), 46.

149 Ellen G. White, *MS 38,* May 1895, Ellen G. White Research Center, Andrews University, Berrien Springs, MI.

150 Ellen G. White, *Ministry of Healing* (Mountain View, CA: Review and Herald, 1963), 128.

[151] Ibid., 126.

[152] Ibid., 144.

[153] Ellen G. White, *Welfare Ministry* (Washington DC.: Review and Herald, 1952), 137.

[154] Ellen G. White, *Welfare Ministry,* Ibid.

[155] Ellen G. White, *Gospel Workers* (Mountain View, CA: Review and Herald, 1963), 188.

[156] Ellen G. White, *Medical Ministry* (Mountain View, CA: Pacific Press, 1963), 301.

[157] Ellen G. White, *Counsels to Parents and Teachers* (Mountain View, CA: Pacific Press, 1963), 521.

[158] Ellen G. White, *Evangelism* (Washington, DC.: Review and Herald, 1970).

[159] Ellen G. White, *Medical Ministry,* 328.

Chapter 12

[160] Sahlin, 21.

[161] Gavin, 10.

BIBLIOGRAPHY

Ackroyd, P. R., A. R. C. Leaney, and J. W. Packer. *The Cambridge Bible Commentary*. Cambridge, Great Britain: Cambridge, 1973.

Allsopp, Bruce. *The Garden Ecology*. New York: New York: Morrow, 1972.

Amazon.Com, "The Origins of the Urban Crisis," Eton Studies in America; available at pc http://www.amazon.com/exec/obides/... goulinemichigana/ 5616-3839785-705781.

Anderson, Rufus. *To Advance the Gospel*. Ed. R. Pierce Beaver. Grand Rapids: Wm. B. Eerdmans Pub. Co., 1967.

Anderson, William E. "The Dilemma of the Socially Minded." *Religion in Life* 8, no. 1 (Winter 1939): Armstrong, Terry A. *Hebrew-English Lexicon of the Old Testament*. Grand Rapids, MI: Zondervan, 1989.

Badillo, Luis. "A Survey of the Social Gospel and Seventh-day Adventist in 1890s and early 1900s." *Review and Herald*, (24 May, 1973): 6.

Banks, Robert. "The Early Church as a Caring Community." *Evangelical Review of Theology*, no. 1, (1983):310–327.

Barnwell, W. H. "Cats in a Wood Stove: Reflections on Building a New Social Gospel Movement." *The Christian Century* 96, no. 1 (1979): 585-588.

Barrett, David B. *World-Class Cities and World Evangelization*. Global Evangelization Movement: The AD 2000 Series., AL: New Hope, 1986.

Beals, Arthur. *Beyond Hunger: A Biblical Mandate for Societal Responsibility*. Portland, OR: Multnomah Press, 1985.

Beaver, R. Pierce, ed. *American Missions in Bicentennial Perspective*. South Pasadena, CA: William Carey Library, 1977.

Bennett, Gail C., ed. *Supporting World Missions in an Age of Change: Selected Addresses and Workshops Presented to the 1983 ACMC North American Conference*. The Role of the Local Church in World Missions Series. Wheaton, IL: The Association of Church Missions Committees, 1984.

Bennett, John C. *Social Salvation*. New York: Charles Scribner's Sons, 1948.

Bennett, John C., ed. *The Local Church: Seedbed for Missions: Selected Addresses and Workshops Presented to the 1981 ACMC North American Conference.*

The Role of the Local Church in World Missions Series. Monrovia, CA: The Association of Church Missions Committees, 1982.

Berry, George R. *The Interlinear Literal Translation of the Hebrew Old Testament.* Grand Rapids, MI: Zondervan, 1943.

"Bible Principle." Silver Spring, MD: North American Division Church Ministries, 1990.

Black, W. G., Jr. "Social work in World War I: A Method Lost." *Social Service Review*, 65, no. 3 (1991): 379-402.

Bosch, David J. *Transforming Mission.* Maryknoll, New York: Orbis Books, 1991.

Bradford, E. E. "Hunger and the Caring Church." *Adventist Review* (15 May, 1988): 17.

Bradshaw, Bruce. *Bridging the Gap.* Monrovia, CA MARC, 1992.

Bühlmann, Walbert. *The Coming of the Third Church: An Analysis of the Present and Future of the Church.* Maryknoll, NY: Orbis Books, 1977.

Butler, Jonathan B. "City of Big Shoulders," *Insight*, (11 August 1970): 14.

Carpenter, J. A. "Fundamentalist Institutions and the Rise of Evangelical Protestantism, 1929–1942." *Church History* 49 (1980): 62-75.

Chilson, Karen Stockton and Mike Preas, "Involvement in Compassion Ministries," Unpublished paper, Walla Walla College, College Place, WA, 1980.

"City of Detroit cited by National Magazine for $17 billion in Economic Growth success," http://www.cildetroit.mi.us/mayors%20release/mr040301.htm.

Bradford, E. "Hunger and the Caring Church," *Adventist Review*, (15 May, 1988): 17.

Coggins, Wade T., and E. L. Frizen, Jr., eds. *Evangelical Missions Tomorrow.* South Pasadena, CA: William Carey Library, 1977.

Cohen, Walter J., "Social Welfare Programs." *The Encyclopedia Americana*, 25: 139.

"Community Church Service," *Social Action* 5 (January 1972).

"Community Programs and Welfare Reform." http://www.acf.dhhs.gov/news/welfare/w.830fdreg.htm, p. 2 of 3 and 3 of 3. 1996.

Conn, Harvie M. *Eternal Word and Changing Worlds: Theology, Anthropology, and Mission in Trialogue.* Grand Rapids, MI: Academe Books (Zondervan), 1984.

Conrad, A. P. "Social Ministry in the Early Church: An Integrated Component of the Christian Community," *Social Thought* 5, no. 23 (Spring 1980): 41.

Copeland, E. Luther. *World Mission and World Survival: The Challenge and Urgency of Global Missions Today.* Nashville: Broadman Press, 1985.

Data Entry, Analysis, Report: Center for Health Research Consulting Group, Loma Linda University, California.

Dunton, Hugh I., Baldur Pfeiffer, and Børge Schantz, eds. *Adventist Missions Facing the 21st Century: A Reader.* Frankfurt am Main: Peter Lang, 1990.

Ellison, Edgar J., ed. *Christian Relief and Development: Developing Workers for Effective Ministry.* Dallas: Word Publishing, 1989.

Elmore, Vernon O. *Layman's Library of Christian Doctrine.* Nashville, TN: Broadman Press, 1986.

Escobar, Donoso and Gary Hutchinson, "The 1996 Social Welfare Reform: What Does It Mean for Family Ministry?" *Journal of Family Ministry* 11 no 2, (Spring 1997): 4.

Ferguson, Sinclair B. et al., "Salvation." *New Dictionary of Theology.* Leicester, England: Intervarsity Press, 1988.

Ferguson, Sinclair B., and David F. Wright, *New Dictionary of Theology.* Avon, Great Britain: The Bath Press, 1988.

Flanagan, Padraig, ed. *A New Missionary Era.* Maryknoll, NY: Orbis Books, 1982.

Furness, George M. *The Social Context of Pastoral Care.* Louisville, Kentucky: Westminster John Knox Press, 1994.

Garland, Diana S., "The Church as a Context for Social Work Practice," *Review and Expositor* 85 (1988): 255.

Garoogian, Rhoda, and Andrews Garoogian, *American Top-Rated Cities: A Statistical Handbar.* Baco Raton, FL: Universal Reference Publication, 1997.

Gavin, John, "Adventist Service" Term paper (27 April 1992): 10.

General Conference of Seventh-day Adventist (Silver Spring, MD), *The Role of Social Ministry in the Seventh-day Adventist Church* (October 10-11, 1977): 2-5.

General Conference of Seventh-day Adventists (Washington DC). *General Conference Bulletin* 2, no. 8 (29 October 1882): 2.

General Conference of Seventh-day Adventist, *God's Creation*, Adult Sabbath School Bible Study Guide, Personal Ministries Department. Napa, ID: Pacific Press, 1999.

Gilliland, Burel E. and Richard K. James. *Handbook of Cognitive Behavioral Therapist*, CA: Brook and Cole Publishing, 1997.

Gilliland, Dean S. *Pauline Theology & Mission Practice*. Grand Rapids: Baker Book House, 1983.

Gorrell, D. K. *The Age of Social Responsibility: The Social Gospel in the Progressive Era 1900–1920*. Macon, GA: Mercer University Press, 1988.

Greenway, Roger S., and Timothy M. Monsma. *Cities: Missions' New Frontier*. Grand Rapids: Baker Book House, 1989.

Grigg, Viv. *Companion to the Poor*. Monrovia, CA: MARC. 1990.

Hiseberger, Jean M. *The Catholic Bible*. New York: Oxford University Press, 1995.

"Hospital Asked to Provide Constant Care for Donor." *The Herald-Palladium*, Benton Harbor, MI, (21October 1988): 7(a).

Johnson, W.G. "Christian in a Need World," *Adventist Review*, (May 1988): 3.

Johnstone, Patrick. *Operation World*. Grand Rapids: Zondervan Publishing House, 1993.

Keil, C. F., and D. F. Delitzsch, *Bible Commentary on the Old Testament*. Grand Rapids, MI: Wm. B. Eerdmans, 1952.

Kidner, Derek. *Genesis*. Chicago: Intervarsity Press, 1967.

King, W. M. "History as Revelation in the Theology of the Social Gospel." *Harvard Theological Review* 76, no. 1 (1987): 109-129.

Directory. Michigan Conference of Seventh-day Adventist. Lansing, Michigan.

Lausanne Occasional Papers. 24 vols. Wheaton, IL: Lausanne Committee for World Evangelization, 1978–83.

Lee, Francis Nigel. *The Origin and Destiny of Man*. Nutley, NJ: Presbyterian and Reformed Press, 1977.

Leiby, J. "Charity Organization Reconsidered." *Social Service Review* 58, no. 4 (1984): 523-538.

Leiby, J. "Moral Foundations of Social Welfare and Social Work: A Historical View". *Social Work* 30, no. 4 (1985): 323-330.

Leighly, John. *Land Life*. Los Angeles, CA: University of California Press, 1963.

Leonard, Bill J. "The Modern Church and Social Action," *Review and Expositor* 85, no. 2 (Spring 1988): 764.

Liebman, David. *The Eternal Torah*. Rivervale, NJ: Pines Press, 1979.

Linder, Marion C. *Nutritional Biochemistry and Metabolism*. New York, 1985.

Lindley, S. "Neglected Voices and Praxis in the Social Gospel." *The Journal of Religious Ethics* 18, no. 1 (1990): 75-99.

Linthicum, Robert C. *Empowering the Poor* Ventura, CA: Ventura Publisher, 1991.

Manser, Nancy. *Lutheran Social Services of Michigan*. Kimcraft Printer, Michigan, 1980.

Mayor's Press Release: City of Detroit Disagrees With Population Estimates Released by U.S. Census Bureau. http://www.c1.detroit. mi.us/mayor%20release/1999releases/m.0701991.htm.

McGavran, Donald A. *Momentous Decisions in Missions Today*. Grand Rapids: Baker Book house, 1984.

Mencher, S. *Poor Law to Poverty Program*. Pittsburgh: University of Pittsburgh Press, 1967.

Miles, Delos, *Evangelism and Social Involvement*, Nashville: Broadman Press, 1986.

Moberg, David O. *The Great Reversal*. Philadelphia, PA: J. B. Lippincott Company, 1977.

Morland, J. P., and David M. Ciocchi, eds *Christian Perspectives on Being Human*. Grand Rapids: Baker Book House, 1973.

National Internet Clearing House (NICH) Welfare Reform at the Federal State, and Local Levels, Wayne County, MI. http://www.com/hp/nwr/ mi26163.html 1997.

New Welfare System will spring from Hopes, Theories, and Myth. Making Welfare Work. A Mercury News Edition. Accessed at http://www. sjmercuy.com/opinion/welfare/edit.html, 28, 1995.

Nicholls, Bruce. *In Word and Deed: Evangelism and Social Responsibility*. Exeter, England: The Paternoster Press, 1985.

Nicholls, William. *Confronting Images of Man*. New York: Seabury Press, 1966.

Niebuhr, H. R., and Yeager, (eds.). "The Social Gospel and the Mind of Jesus." *The Journal of Religious Ethics*, 16, no. 1 (1988): 109-127.

Oosterwal, Gottfried, R. Staples, W.B. Douglas, and R.E. Turner. *Servants for Christ: The Adventist Church Facing the '80s*. Berrien Springs, MI: Andrews University Press, 1980.

Payne, Malcolm. *Modern Social Work Theory*. Chicago, IL: Lyceum Books, 1997.

Price, R. M. "A Fundamentalist Social Gospel?" *The Christian Century* 96, no. 2 (1997): 1183-1186.

Rad, Gerhard von. *Genesis*. Philadelphia: The Sem Press, 1972.

Rauschenbusch, Walter. *A Theology for Social Gospel*. New York: Abingdon Press, 1917.

Richardson, William J. *Social Action vs. Evangelism*. CA William Carey Library, 1977.

Richmond Garland, Diana S. "The Church as a Context for Social Work Practice," *Review and Expositor* 85 (1988): 255.

Rock, Calvin. "Did Ellen White Downplay Social Work?" *Adventist Review*, (May 15, 1988): 6.

Rosado, Caleb "The Nature of Society and the Challenge to Mission," *International Review of Mission* 77 (January 1988): 35.

Rose, N. E. "Work Relief in the 1930s and the Origins of the Social Security Act," *Social Services Review* 63, no. 1 (1989): 61-91.

Sachs, John R. *The Christian Vision of Humanity*. Minneapolis: The Liturgical Press, 1991.

Sahlin, Monte "Adventist Community Services," *Adventist Review* (5 May 1988): 21.

Scherer, James A., and Stephen B. Bevans, eds. *New Directions in Mission & Evangelization*. Maryknoll, NY: Orbis Books, 1992.

Schwarz, Richard W. "Adventist's Social Gospel Advocate, John Harvey Kellogg," *Spectrum*, (Spring 1969): 5-28.

Seventh-day Adventist Bible Dictionary. Edited by Siegfried H. Horn. Washington DC: Review and Herald Pub. Assn., 1960 s.v., "Genesis."

Sherman, Amy L. "A Call for Church Welfare Reform," *Christianity Today* (October 6), 1997.

Sider, Ronald J. *One-sided Christianity* Grand Rapids: Zondervan Publishing House, 1993.

Sine, Tom, ed. *The Church in Response to Human Need*. Monrovia, CA: MARC, 1983.

Smith, L. A. "The Hopelessness of the Effort to Reform Politics," *Review and Herald* (6 April, 1905): 5.

Snyder, Howard A., with Daniel V. Runyan. *Foresight: 10 Major Trends That Will Dramatically Affect the Future of Christians and the Church.* Nashville: Thomas Nelson Publishers, 1986.

"Social Security: Social Insurance," found at http://www.cas.michco.edu/ security/tour6.htm.

Stott, John R. W. *Christian Mission in the Modern World.* Downers Grove, IL: Intervarsity Press, 1975.

Sun Herald Online (Internet), Smith "Church Finds a Vision in Traditional Role of Social Services," http://www.sunherald.com/living/docs/ vision0215.htm, by Marquita Smith, 193.

"The Fabulous Ruins of Detroit"; available at http://www.bhhere.com/ ruins/industry/default.htm, p. 1 of 1.

The New International Dictionary of the Bible. Grand Rapid, Michigan: Press-Zondervan Publishing House, 1978: s.v., "Genesis."

Tyner, Mitchell A. "The Church and Society," *Adventist Review*, (4 January 1990): 14-15.

"Unemployment rises in nearly all of Michigan," http://www.freep.com. news/Latestnews/pm2269_20010307.htm.

Unger, Merrill F. *Unger's Commentary on the Old Testament*, vol. 1. New York: Doubleday & Company, 1975.

Vine, W. E. *Dictionary of Bible Words.* Nashville, TN: Thomas Nelson 1999.

Vine, W. E., Merrill F. Unger, and William White, Jr. *Vine's Complete Expository Dictionary of Old and New Testament Words*, Nashville, TN: Thomas Nelson, 1985.

Warden, I.L., "Cities," *Adventist Review*, (May 5 1998): 13.

Webster's Collegiate Dictionary, 10th edition. Springfield, Mass. Merriam-Webster. s.v., "Assessment." 1997: 69.

White Jr., Ronald C. "Social Reform and the Social Gospel in America," *Commission on the Church's Participation in Development.* Switzerland: Imprimerie Le Concorde, n.d.

White, E. G. *Counsels to Parents and Teachers.* Mountain View, CA: Pacific Press, 1963.

White, E. G. *Evangelism.* Washington, DC: Review and Herald, 1970.

White, E. G. *Gospel Workers*, Mountain View, CA: Review and Herald, 1963.

White, E. G. *Medical Ministry*, Mountain View, CA: Pacific Press Publisher, 1963.

White, E. G. *Ministry of Healing*, Mountain View, CA: Review and Herald, 1963.

White, E. G. *MS 38*, May 1895. Ellen G. White Research Center, Andrews University, Berrien Springs, MI.

White, E. G. *Pastoral Ministry*. Old Columbia Pike, Silver Spring, MD, 1995

White, E. G. *Patriarchs and Prophets*, Mountain View, CA: Review and Herald, 1958.

White, E. G. *Welfare Ministry*, Washington DC: Review and Herald Publishing Association, 1952.

White, Edward W. *Significant Issues for the 1970s*. Philadelphia: Fortress Press, 1970.

White, R. C., Jr. *Liberty and Justice for All: Racial Reform and the Social Gospel, 1877–1925*. San Francisco, CA: Harper Row, 1990.

White, Ronald C., and Howard C. Hopkins, *The Social Gospel*. Philadelphia, PA: Temple University Press, 1976.

Widmer, Myron. "What the Adventist Church is Doing about Poverty," *Adventist Review* (May 1988): 19.

Wilmore, Gayround S. *The Secular Relevance of the Church*. Philadelphia, PA: The Westminster Press, 1952.

Wilson, William. *Old Testament Word Studies*. McLean, VA: Macdonald Publisher, 137.

Wilson, Nelson. "Global Strategy and the Poor," *Adventist Review*, (May 1988): 5

Ziegler, Ekhard E., and L. J. Filer, Jr. *Present Knowledge in Nutrition*. Washington DC: International Life Science Institute Press, 1996.

Appendix

Practical Application

Appendix I

Practical Application
Training Recommendation

The need for faith-based socioeconomic development and social entrepreneurship training is supported by the majority of respondents showing a positive response for faith-based socioeconomic development and social entrepreneurship in 21st century.

The study shows different services are provided in all churches that participated in the study in Detroit, Michigan.

The faith-based social ministry programs of the church target five areas of services

Social services are provided at most community service centers and many local churches. These include dispensing clothing, bedding, food, furniture, and household items, along with job referral assistance.

Health services may include visiting the sick, home nursing, health screening, van ministries, health fairs, clinics, and hospital visits.

Services to children include foster care, volunteer grand-parenting, day and summer camps, and big brother/big sister programs.

Inner city programs include shelters for the homeless, soup kitchens, social service centers, and other antipoverty activities.

Other services include group sessions for victims of violence, grief, and alcohol abuse, drug recovery programs, parenting classes, and behavioral centers.

For all practical purposes, an attempt to implement faith-based socioeconomic development and social entrepreneurship training cannot be overemphasized. Therefore, setting up faith-based socioeconomic development and social entrepreneurship in the community for the community will requires putting in place eight basic steps:

Step 1. A theology of holistic ministry should be developed that will address each of the natural resources identified in this study and how members can get involve and take responsibility investing in their development as part of their dominion responsibility especially in cities, towns and part of the world where there is lack of mention, concern or investment to develop natural resources for basic needs and use. Also, the church will have to develop a sound theology of self as the image and likeness of God rejecting all efforts and conducts in the past to teach or represent efforts to degrade another recognizing all mankind are created to have dominion over the earth and the resources created by God in compliance with the intent of God for all succeeding generation of Adam and Eve. The church will also have to develop a theology of labor and rest emphasizing both and implementing both as one in compliance with the divine command. This basic teaching will have to be included in training, belief and service in the church and outside the church.

Step 2. Members in each church community should develop a demographic analysis of their community for better understanding of their own environment and location on the earth for dominion responsibility not just inside the church. They should set-up a committee responsible to assess the church community. Obtain a map and note the location of the church. A radius of six miles from the church will indicate the church community in an urban setting. A church in a suburban area would use a nine-mile radius.

Step 3. The population distribution within the circle needs to be determined.

Go to the city or county office and seek help to estimate the population in the target area; additional information may be available on the Internet. The children within the targeted community should be identified by ethnic distribution, parents' occupations, etc.

Step 4. The committee needs to identify the specific social needs or problems associated with each population group within the area.

It would be very useful to identify trends in employment and unemployment, the distribution of the workforce between males and females, the distribution of income, and the cost for housing, medical care, utilities, teen pregnancy, homelessness, hunger, poor neighborhoods, poor housing, school dropout rates, and alcohol and drug dependencies.

Step 5. Social service leaders should seek sources of change and consider the best conversion agents.

The people, groups, or institutions that control human resources, such as land, other materials, and industrial and information resources, must be identified. Institutions that are agents of values and change should be designated, and people in social positions—such as ministers of religion and people in other professions who are concerned primarily with the interpretation of values and who wield power by virtue of their right to make value judgments—should be recognized.

Step 6. Those affected by the problem may help to find a solution. The most widely prevalent social units for participation and individual change are religious organizations.

They can tell the church committee what they are doing about the problem in the identified areas. The problems are then presented to the local church so that members can organize a conference or dialogue.

People from other agencies in the area who have already had success in working on the problems should be invited to share what they have learned. The church should develop a list of interested volunteers who would like to work on the problems that have been identified.

Step 7. Other agencies in the area should be visited.

Visiting other agencies will provide information about how they organize, what resources they use, and how they operate their programs in the local community. A careful study of this information is very helpful.

Step 8. By this time the church will be prepared to develop programs and to decide which services it can provide. The church can review the list of resources and problems identified in chapter eight and nine that needs investment and development or new programs and services to address social problems in their community.

Following those steps will enable the church to coordinate with existing services (i.e., relating to present services and preventing overlapping), to extend present services, to initiate new services that meet the community's needs, and to respond to specific problems.

The work is started by writing out the problems for a problem index that can be used to develop long- and short-term goals, a plan of action, a target date, and a completion date.

The action plan could be a group of specific programs or services focused on addressing specific problems. These should be advertised in the media, in churches around the community, and at other agencies.

An open house can be planned; this can supply practical benefits to church leaders who need help or ideas of an outline for community social ministry training.

In response to the need for faith-based socioeconomic development and social entrepreneurship training in the community. I have added a course description outline for practical training purposes.

Community Social Ministry Training

3 Credits
Time: 9:00 AM to 5:00 PM
Room:
Instructor:
Phone:

Course Description

This training will provide Biblical and practical skills to participants to the role of human identity in the control of created resources and solving human problems in the community. Participants will develop practical skills for identifying untapped resources, develop programs and services for socioeconomic development and social entrepreneurship as a Biblical mandate in keeping with human identity and dominion.

The course is intended to focus on the theoretical perspective of man in his environment before and after the fall and the theories of how to encounter and prepare man in his modern environment to self improve, exercise dominion and solve problems. Participants will discuss the influence of theoretical dichotomy or dualism on Christian ministry and the material and spiritual mandate of the church.

Participants will develop basic skills for analyzing a person using holistic theory models. Participants will develop skills in planning interventions. Specific examples from churches in Detroit will be used in the presentation.

Prerequisite

Interest in helping people experience wholeness and recovery.

Selected Reading:

Rad., Gerhard von. *Genesis*. Philadelphia: The Sem. Press, 1972

Vine, W. E. Merrill F. Unger and William White, Jr. *Vine's Complete Expository Dictionary of Old and New Testament Words*. Nashville, TN: Thomas Nelson, 1985.

Bradshaw, Bruce. *Bridging the Gap*. Monrovia, CA: MARC, 1992.

Mayor's Press Release: City of Detroit Disagrees With Population Estimates Released by U.S. Census Bureau. http://www.c1.detroit.mi.us/mayor%20release/1999releases/m.0701991.htm.

McGavran, Donald A. *Momentous Decisions in Missions Today.* Grand Rapids: Baker Book house, 1984.

Mencher, S. *Poor Law to Poverty Program.* Pittsburgh: University of Pittsburgh Press, 1967.

Miles, Delos, *Evangelism and Social Involvement,* Nashville: Broadman Press, 1986.

Moberg, David O. *The Great Reversal.* Philadelphia, PA: J. B. Lippincott Company, 1977.

Morland, J. P., and David M. Ciocchi, eds *Christian Perspectives on Being Human.* Grand Rapids: Baker Book House, 1973.

National Internet Clearing House (NICH) Welfare Reform at the Federal State, and Local Levels, Wayne County, MI. http://www.com/hp/nwr/mi26163.html 1997.

New Welfare System will spring from Hopes, Theories, and Myth. Making Welfare Work. A Mercury News Edition. Accessed at http://www.sjmercuy.com/opinion/welfare/edit.html, 28, 1995.

Nicholls, Bruce. *In Word and Deed: Evangelism and Social Responsibility.* Exeter, England: The Paternoster Press, 1985.

Nicholls, William. *Confronting Images of Man.* New York: Seabury Press, 1966.

Niebuhr, H. R., and Yeager, (eds.). "The Social Gospel and the Mind of Jesus." *The Journal of Religious Ethics,* 16, no. 1 (1988): 109-127.

Oosterwal, Gottfried, R. Staples, W.B. Douglas, and R.E. Turner. *Servants for Christ: The Adventist Church Facing the '80s.* Berrien Springs, MI: Andrews University Press, 1980.

Payne, Malcolm. *Modern Social Work Theory.* Chicago, IL: Lyceum Books, 1997.

Price, R. M. "A Fundamentalist Social Gospel?" *The Christian Century* 96, no. 2 (1997): 1183-1186.

Rad, Gerhard von. *Genesis.* Philadelphia: The Sem Press, 1972.

Rauschenbusch, Walter. *A Theology for Social Gospel.* New York: Abingdon Press, 1917.

Richardson, William J. *Social Action vs. Evangelism.* CA William Carey Library, 1977.

Richmond Garland, Diana S. "The Church as a Context for Social Work Practice," *Review and Expositor* 85 (1988): 255.

Rock, Calvin. "Did Ellen White Downplay Social Work?" *Adventist Review,* (May 15, 1988): 6.

Rosado, Caleb "The Nature of Society and the Challenge to Mission," *International Review of Mission* 77 (January 1988): 35.

Rose, N. E. "Work Relief in the 1930s and the Origins of the Social Security Act," *Social Services Review* 63, no. 1 (1989): 61-91.

Sachs, John R. *The Christian Vision of Humanity*. Minneapolis: The Liturgical Press, 1991.

Sahlin, Monte "Adventist Community Services," *Adventist Review* (5 May 1988): 21.

Scherer, James A., and Stephen B. Bevans, eds. *New Directions in Mission & Evangelization*. Maryknoll, NY: Orbis Books, 1992.

Schwarz, Richard W. "Adventist's Social Gospel Advocate, John Harvey Kellogg," *Spectrum*, (Spring 1969): 5-28.

Seventh-day Adventist Bible Dictionary. Edited by Siegfried H. Horn. Washington DC: Review and Herald Pub. Assn., 1960 s.v., "Genesis."

Sherman, Amy L. "A Call for Church Welfare Reform," *Christianity Today* (October 6), 1997.

Sider, Ronald J. *One-sided Christianity* Grand Rapids: Zondervan Publishing House, 1993.

Sine, Tom, ed. *The Church in Response to Human Need*. Monrovia, CA: MARC, 1983.

Smith, L. A. "The Hopelessness of the Effort to Reform Politics," *Review and Herald* (6 April, 1905): 5.

Snyder, Howard A., with Daniel V. Runyan. *Foresight: 10 Major Trends That Will Dramatically Affect the Future of Christians and the Church*. Nashville: Thomas Nelson Publishers, 1986.

"Social Security: Social Insurance," found at http://www.cas.michco.edu/security/tour6.htm.

Stott, John R. W. *Christian Mission in the Modern World*. Downers Grove, IL: Intervarsity Press, 1975.

Sun Herald Online (Internet), Smith "Church Finds a Vision in Traditional Role of Social Services," http://www.sunherald.com/living/docs/vision0215.htm, by Marquita Smith, 193.

"The Fabulous Ruins of Detroit"; available at http://www.bhhere.com/ruins/industry/default.htm, p. 1 of 1.

The New International Dictionary of the Bible. Grand Rapid, Michigan: Press-Zondervan Publishing House, 1978: s.v., "Genesis."

Tyner, Mitchell A. "The Church and Society," *Adventist Review*, (4 January 1990): 14-15.

"Unemployment rises in nearly all of Michigan," http://www.freep.com.news/Latestnews/pm2269_20010307.htm.

Unger, Merrill F. *Unger's Commentary on the Old Testament*, vol. 1. New York: Doubleday & Company, 1975.

Vine, W. E. *Dictionary of Bible Words*. Nashville, TN: Thomas Nelson 1999.

Vine, W. E., Merrill F. Unger, and William White, Jr. *Vine's Complete Expository Dictionary of Old and New Testament Words*, Nashville, TN: Thomas Nelson, 1985.

Warden, I.L., "Cities," *Adventist Review*, (May 5 1998): 13.

Webster's Collegiate Dictionary, 10th edition. Springfield, Mass. Merriam-Webster. s.v., "Assessment." 1997: 69.

White Jr., Ronald C. "Social Reform and the Social Gospel in America," *Commission on the Church's Participation in Development*. Switzerland: Imprimerie Le Concorde, n.d.

White, E. G. *Counsels to Parents and Teachers*. Mountain View, CA: Pacific Press, 1963.

White, E. G. *Evangelism*. Washington, DC: Review and Herald, 1970.

White, E. G. *Gospel Workers*, Mountain View, CA: Review and Herald, 1963.

White, E. G. *Medical Ministry*, Mountain View, CA: Pacific Press Publisher, 1963.

White, E. G. *Ministry of Healing*, Mountain View, CA: Review and Herald, 1963.

White, E. G. *MS 38*, May 1895. Ellen G. White Research Center, Andrews University, Berrien Springs, MI.

White, E. G. *Pastoral Ministry*. Old Columbia Pike, Silver Spring, MD, 1995

White, E. G. *Patriarchs and Prophets*, Mountain View, CA: Review and Herald, 1958.

White, E. G. *Welfare Ministry*, Washington DC: Review and Herald Publishing Association, 1952.

White, Edward W. *Significant Issues for the 1970s*. Philadelphia: Fortress Press, 1970.

White, R. C., Jr. *Liberty and Justice for All: Racial Reform and the Social Gospel, 1877–1925*. San Francisco, CA: Harper Row, 1990.

White, Ronald C., and Howard C. Hopkins, *The Social Gospel*. Philadelphia, PA: Temple University Press, 1976.

Widmer, Myron. "What the Adventist Church is Doing about Poverty," *Adventist Review* (May 1988): 19.

Wilmore, Gayround S. *The Secular Relevance of the Church*. Philadelphia, PA: The Westminster Press, 1952.

Wilson, William. *Old Testament Word Studies*. McLean, VA: Macdonald Publisher, 137.

Wilson, Nelson. "Global Strategy and the Poor," *Adventist Review*, (May 1988): 5

Ziegler, Ekhard E., and L. J. Filer, Jr. *Present Knowledge in Nutrition*. Washington DC: International Life Science Institute Press, 1996.